The
YOUTH
of My YEARS

The YOUTH *of My* YEARS

ALICE TIPTON

Kravitz & Sons
INNOVATORS IN PUBLISHING, MARKETING AND ADVERTISING

Kravitz and Sons LLC
1301 Farmville Blvd, Suite 104
Greenville, NC 27834

Published by Kravitz and Sons LLC.

ISBN: 979-8-89639-261-3 (sc)
ISBN: 979-8-89639-262-0 (e)

Library of Congress Control Number: 2025909382

TABLE OF CONTENTS

ILLUSTRATIONS

i

To my father, for all he did to rear us in those years and because he meant so much to me.

PREFACE

As I wrote this book, I thought a lot about my father. He was an outstanding person, who lived his Christian life and set a good example for his children. I dedicate this book in his memory.

As children in the 1930s and 1940s, growing up together we knew our roots. Although we came from the same household, we all had our own ideas and outlooks on life; therefore, I wrote this book from my own viewpoint about the ins and outs of growing up on the farm in Foster City.

Alice Tipton

CHAPTER ONE
THE SWANSON FAMILY

As I sit here writing, it is my intention to answer my daughters' questions about the time when I was young. I have tried to tell them about my life as a child on a farm, how my family lived without all the modern conveniences of today (it's hard for them to imagine), and how, as a family, we pulled together in order to make it.

To understand better, I tried to imagine how it must have been in Sweden for my father as a little boy. He was from a family of six, and he had three brothers: Ray, Knute, and Eric. He came from the small town of Smoland, which was a little farming community tucked away in the hills. It had giant shade trees in the summer and a thick blanket of snow during the harsh winters.

But they were hardy people who were used to a hard existence, but like some other families who wanted a better life, they wished to migrate to America. Magnus Swanson, my grandfather, was among the first Swedes to come to the United States. He settled in a little town called Foster City, which is in Michigan's Upper Peninsula, and he remained there the rest of his life.

Grandpa was a big man who was used to hard work, so it wasn't long before he found work as a lumberjack. Most men in that area in those days were lumberjacks.

In November 1918, a few years after Grandpa's arrival in the United States, Grandma and the four boys left Smoland for America. They boarded a ship for the states after saying their last goodbyes to their many friends and relatives. Immigration was a big decision on the part of the families who left for the unknown country. Chances were good they would never be able to return to Sweden even for a visit. Most would not have the means.

Dad, along with his mother and brothers, arrived in New York on Christmas Eve. They's had to sail around the war zone, so the trip took longer than usual. Once they arrived, they had to remain on board the ship until December 26, since everything was closed over the holidays. They passed through Ellis Island, then boarded a train for the last leg of the trip to Michigan.

I can imagine how excited they must have been as they rode through the countryside to the Upper Peninsula where Grandpa awaited them and they would become a family once again.

Grandma was a strong Christian, and she held the family together as most mothers do. She'd had it hard rearing four boys in Sweden through those lean years. She didn't sing in the church choir or preach on a street corner, but everyone knew she was a Christian by how she lived her life. She set a pattern for generations to come.

Grandma never learned English; she never felt the need. I suppose she never learned because there were mostly Swedish families living in Foster City, and many of the older people didn't bother to learn. As long as they kept to themselves, as most did, they saw no need.

Once settled, Dad and his brothers started school. They were teased because they could not speak English. Being the new kids in town didn't help either, and they had to prove themselves. Kids can be so harsh to newcomers, and they don't even realize it.

During those early years in America, a girl, Dad's only sister, Anna, was born to the Swanson family. She was very pretty with her long black hair. Then another boy, Oscar, was born.

But things weren't happy for long. One day while playing, Anna fell on the cement steps in front of the school and suffered a severe head injury. She was rushed to a hospital forty miles away, but she never recovered. A short time later, she passed away. Her passing was a great loss to the family because she was the only daughter.

The life of Dad's youngest brother, Oscar, was also cut short. He contracted tuberculosis and died in his twenties. The two deaths caused the family to find comfort in God and each other. The remaining four sons grew up to be lumberjacks like their father.

I don't know much about my mother's side of the family other than she had two brothers, George and Martin. The three of them were born in the Felch area. Mom spent the largest share of her life there, except for the few years she worked in Chicago. Many of the young girls went to work in the big cities, since the only jobs around the Felch area were logging and farming or getting married and rearing a family, which most of the young women did eventually.

My mother's maiden name was Omen. Her father was a gentle man who always wore a smile and had a story to tell as long as there was someone around to listen. He worked for the Ford Motor Company in Iron Mountain, which had since closed its doors. Iron Mountain was the biggest city in the immediate area, and it still is today.

Grandma Omen was always busy helping anyone in need. She was very community minded. She had a smile and kind word for everyone who passed her way. My mother inherited many of those wonderful traits and passed them on to us.

Both of my grandmothers were great cooks and bakers, without a cookbook, of course. They kept us well fed. They measured the ingredients by using a pinch of this and a dash of that. Best of all, everything turned out fit for a king, even when they baked in the old woodstoves. Keeping the oven temperature regulated was a feat in itself. Grandma Swanson brought a lot of recipes from Sweden, which were stored in her head. I can still close my eyes and see a dish of steaming hot Swedish Kringle's and headcheese, which to me was the best in the country.

When my parents were married, they settled on their first farm just outside of town. A few years later, they moved across town to the place where they grew up. It overlooked Foster City, which was nestled in a valley amidst rolling hills on all sides. When we came along, most of the families farmed. Years before, logging had been the main industry.

I lived in Foster City throughout my youth, and even today I like to think of it as my hometown. I have traveled a lot through the years, but I'll always have a soft spot in my heart for Foster City. It is approached on Highway 59, the only road that goes through town.

With a population of 150 people, Foster City is a place where everybody knows everybody and there's a thin line between being concerned and being nosy.

When I was growing up, everyone was always ready and willing to help at the drop of a hat, and that was important to us. The problems of the world rarely got a hold of folks. They were more interested in the people around them. Now, don't misunderstand, they always kept informed about world events, but Foster City was so peaceful and serene, it was like a picture in a storybook.

Like a lot of towns, Foster City had its history. As the lumber mills came and went, some of the people remained. The mills were built in the heart of town, along the banks of the Sturgeon River. Rivers played an important role in the lumber industry because they were used to float the logs from the woods to the mills. In addition, loggers dammed up the waterways to make holding ponds. Foster City had been named for Alonzo Foster, the foreman of the Herman Lumber Company.

Other mills came and went throughout the history of Foster City. One of the best-remembered mills was Morgan Lumber Company, which was the last in a long line of companies. Before leaving the area, Morgan Lumber Company sold the mill and its other holdings, most of Foster City, to the Peterson family. In turn, the Petersons sold a lot of farming land and hired some of the men to log the rest of the timber. Dad was one of the men who worked for the Petersons. He worked on their dairy farm while he worked to build his own homestead. He milked their cows every morning and night, and in between he came home to work on his own farm.

Along with the mills came the railroad, which has since disappeared. In the early years, it came through town at least once a day. The Felch Flyer was used to haul lumber and passengers. A lot of people took the train since travel by horse and buggy was slow. The railroad was named after the town of Felch, which was the largest town on the line. It was a reliable mode of transportation during the time all the men in the towns were busy with logging. Cars were just coming on the scene, and few families could afford them.

Eventually, the last of the timber was about to be harvested, and the town came to a crossroads in its existence. Would it become part of a farming community, or would it die like a lot of other towns that just folded up when the timber was gone. Some of the families moved on with the sawmills, others remained and turned Foster City into a farming community.

The Swansons were among the families that chose to stay behind and farm. We were from a long line of farmers, which stemmed all the way back to the days in Sweden. The Swansons had farmed during the warm summer months, and when the crops were in, they turned to logging to earn a living through the winter. The Swedish people were ideal for the climate and way of life in the Upper Peninsula, logging and farming side by side.

The Petersons not only owned most of the town, they possessed and operated the general store and the one and only gas station, which stood next to each other. These establishments were unique. The station offered full service and served ice cream from buckets kept in a cooler. We could choose the flavor we desired, and Manley, the station owner, would dish it up on a cone. The station had a friendly atmosphere.

The general store was everything its name implied; it sold food, hardware, and everything in between.

Along with the Petersons, the Milligans were one of the earliest families to settle in the area. They operated the post office, which was in the corner of the general store. Pat was the postmaster for years, which, as a kid, seemed like forever. We all had post office boxes because there were no local mail deliveries. The Milligans were also the caretakers of the local Roman Catholic church.

As we traveled through Foster City, we saw two churches. The first was the Swedish Covenant Church, which our family attended, and the other was the Roman Catholic church. Both churches were among the first buildings to be built when people had moved into the area many years before. They were old-fashioned, in our modern-day thinking, but with their steeples and large, unlocked, open doors that faced the road, they welcomed anyone passing.

The school was a stone's throw away, and it was named after Mr. Longfellow. It was a two-story building with an old bell tower. Dad and his brothers attended classes there. There were four classrooms on the main floor. In the basement were the kindergarten classroom and a lunchroom that served hot food. The restrooms were also located in the basement, along with one of the biggest furnaces I have ever seen. It heated the school during those long winters, which seemed to last the whole nine months.

There is no town without a resting place, and our town was no different. The cemetery was located along the hillside, and it was surrounded by a white picket fence. Most, if not all, of the families in Foster City had at least one loved one who had been laid to rest there. Everyone took an interest in how the cemetery looked and worked hard to keep it clean and neat. Each spring, every family in town went out to clean up their lots.

Foster City also had a cheese factory. The farmers sent their raw milk to the factory to be processed, which was an important part of farm life.

There was also a town hotel, one of the first to be built. It was located on the side of the hill overlooking the town and mills. It was torn down when I was quite young, so I don't remember much about it. Since the mills took up most of the flat land along the river, the other buildings, and there were many, were erected around them on the hillsides.

If a person took the county road about a mile out of Foster City and made a sharp turn left, he or she would be traveling on our road, which was rough and crooked. Arrival on top of the hill would reveal our home. It was a big, white, two-story house with a porch across the front and farm buildings in the background.

The kitchen was on the main floor, along with the living and dining rooms and master bedroom. Upstairs were three bedrooms where children slept.

In the basement was a big wood furnace. A grate was in the middle of the living room, just above the furnace, and a smaller grate was located in the ceiling and upstairs floor above. This setup served as our central heating system.

The kitchen had no modern conveniences. We hauled water and wood for cooking. During the summer, the kitchen would be too hot from the cookstove, but its heat made it cozy in the kitchen during the winter.

We had no bathtub, so the kitchen served as a place to bathe, too. We heated the water on the stove, then poured it into the big tub in the middle of the floor. This ritual took place every Saturday night. We didn't have a sink, either, so we had to wash and rinse dishes in pans of water on the kitchen table. This routine reminds me of the times we went camping, but it was a daily chore as I grew up. Years later, my daughter asked, "When you were young, did you do a lot of camping?" To me, it wasn't much fun, and it wasn't camping.

We had no indoor plumbing, so we used the little house on the back forty with a little half moon window. There was no heat, which made it rough in the winter. We spent the least amount of time there as possible. In the summer, it was a different story because it was so hot outside. The building was next to the woods, and it was shaded. We never had toilet paper, so we used the old Sears and Wards catalogs instead.

The main barn, which was located at the north end, had a hayloft above and housed the cattle. The horse barn was built later, and it was attached to the main barn. Dad also built a chicken coop, pigpens, and a woodshed. Most of the time, however, the woodshed held the farm machinery instead of wood. Next to the other building was the grainery. It had silos to store the silage each fall.

Every few years, we whitewashed our buildings. I called the whitewash watered down paint. It didn't last long, but it went on the buildings easily, and it was cheap.

A farm was a great place to rear six kids, even if it was a hard life. It was fun, along with the work.

New families moved into town, and they needed medical care. We had the best nurse around, right there in Foster City. We all called her Nurse Carlson. She was always available when needed, whether it was to deliver babies or treat someone for an accident or illness. She performed wonderful service for the community, without much thanks at times, and we all remembered her. Years later, the town commemorated her for her contributions to the people of Foster City and the surrounding areas by making her Citizen of the Year. I don't know how much training she had, but it didn't matter. She did the job, and she did it well.

Nurse Carlson delivered most of the children in that area because the hospital was so far away. Most of the babies were born at home, which was very risky. If complications set in and a hospital was needed, there was no time to get there. So it was up to Nurse Carlson to do the best she could, along with a lot of prayers.

The nearest hospital was at Iron Mountain, which was about 40 miles away, and that was like traveling 160 miles today.

When a baby was on the way, there wasn't much time to get help because we had no phones. Someone in the family would have to jump into a car or a truck, whatever was available, and run out to the Carlson farm to bring her.

Nurse Carlson and her husband were farmers, along with the rest of us. They had three children. She was always a busy woman, but she seemed to have time for the rest of the town. As I look back, I think of the many times she must have been tired, but she never said no to anyone. The Lord was with her for her to keep going as she did.

Many of the children made it through birth, but even if there were no problems at the beginning, pneumonia got a good number of them before they reached the age of three. When a child developed pneumonia, there wasn't much anyone could do. There were no shots like today. Prayer helped then, and prayer can and would help today if we used if more and did not totally depend on medicine.

Mom and Dad were about to start their own family, and in the years to come, they were great parents. People never fully understand the role of their parents until they have children of their own. At that time, a person pays for his or her upbringing of sorts. Since I have girls of my own today, I understand what my parents went through. Times were very different from today.

Dad was a slender man with brown eyes and hair. He wore a determined look, and he had no room for foolishness. He always finished what he started. There was no turning back once he began a project. As the years passed, I became thankful for this quality in him.

Mom was a large woman with lovely black hair and dark eyes, just the opposite of Dad. She had a great personality, which she inherited from her mother. She was understanding but firm. Even now, I can close my eyes and visualize her playing the guitar and singing under the apple tree in the backyard as if it were yesterday. Mom is no longer with us, and my memories are few, but what I do remember, I greatly cherish.

Marion was the first child to come along. She was born in February and looked like Mom. She had the same pleasant personality. Through the years, she was a sickly child, but she was God sent. She turned out to be a pillar of the community. She was a great inspiration, and I always knew her prayers were with me. Later in life, she married Kenneth Johnson, and they settled in Foster City. They had three lovely children: Judy, Gordy, and Gary. Marion made a difference as she walked through life, even if it were just in her own little corner of the world. I can truly say she was one of God's instruments in his service.

Next on the scene was John, a boy who was born in July and whose biblical name suited him well. He was different from Marion. He was lightly complected like Dad and had the same determination and drive. After graduating from high school, he served in the army in Germany. He later married Joyce from Niagara, and they settled there. They, too, had three children: Paul, Rochelle, and Perer. John was his own person, and he reflected God in his life. He was hardworking and honest. I always respected him for his beliefs and values. He became very active in his local church, and he set a fine example for those around him.

In early September, Anna arrived. She looked a lot like Mom and Marion, but she had a mind of her own, which proved to be a great asset through the years even though having a mind of your own in those days wasn't the best idea. She, too, had a deep inner faith. She was well liked and fun to be around. She always seemed to do the right thing while she was growing up, as did Marion and Johnny. I guess I was a little envious during that time. When Anna left home to be on her own, she went into the medical field. Later, she married a local doctor, Edward McCormack. They had a daughter, Roxann, and they, too, settled in the Niagara area.

Then came Ruthie, just before Christmas. She was light complected like John and Dad. Ruthie was the one who never got into trouble. It seemed she never disobeyed, which is hard to believe but true. She loved to go to church and had a deep faith in God. Mom and Dad made sure we all developed deep faith so that when we became adults, we would have a good foundation on which to build our lives. Ruthie, too, went into the medical field. She served in the air force as a nurse, and she later married Joe. Ruthie didn't return to the local area to live. She and Joe settled in Louisiana.

On April 7, 1936, after a cold winter and during the coming of spring, I was born into the Swanson family. When I came along, I didn't look like Anna or Marion with their dark hair and beautiful eyes, nor did I look like Johnny or Ruthie. You might say I had a look of my own. I had red, curly hair. I was skinny and on the ugly side. Too bad I didn't stay skinny, but good things don't last forever.

Through my early years, I was teased a lot about my red hair by my sisters and brothers and at school. I had trouble doing the right thing. It seemed I was in trouble all the time. One reason I got into trouble was because I didn't listen very well to my parents-but I learned.

The last Swanson to arrive was Wallin. He arrived in the summer, in the middle of June. He was dark complected like Mom, Marion, and Anna. Because he was the youngest, at times I thought he was spoiled, but as he grew up, he shared the work on the farm like the rest of us. He turned out to be the farmer of the family and remained at home unlike the rest of us who moved on when we grew up and were on our own. Wallin later married Carol, a local girl, and they had four children: Joellen, David, Greg, and Glenda. Their family was also very active in the church. In later years, Wallin and his family moved to Springhill, Tennessee.

All through our childhood, we attended Sunday school at the Swedish Covenant Church. Our parents set us on the right road, and if we strayed, we always came back to God. As we went through life, I like to think we helped someone along the way and that we made a difference in this world.

1890-1980. The Swanson home in Sweden.
Grandma, Dad, Eric, Knute, and Grandpa

Our country store and post office

Swedish Covenant Church

Roman Catholic church and our grade school

Foster City in the 1920s and 1930s

Logging in the winter during the early days in Foster City

Sawmill in Foster City (1920s)

Our homestead

Our home, summer and winter

Cows on the farm

Memorial Day

Our mother's grave

Ann

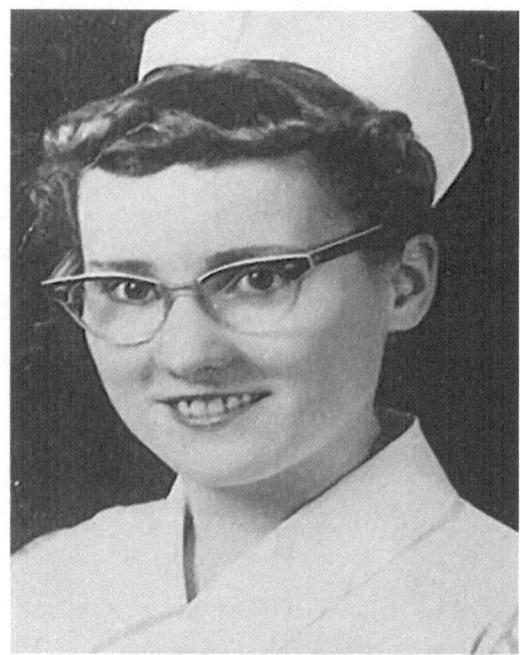

Ruthie

Wally and Carol (his wife). Their daughter, Jo Ellen

Daughter Roxanne

Mom and Dad

Johnny, Ruthie, Grandma, Me, Ann, and Marion

Johnny and Joyce

Marion and her family

The girls at church camp

Mom in the late 1920s

Grandpa and Grandma's fiftieth wedding anniversary: 1952

Ration cards from my husband's family

CHAPTER TWO
MY FIRST STEPS

With our family complete, we were about to embark on life's road. The first thing was to have a good foundation on which to grow. After parents lay the foundation for their children, it is up to the offspring to build on it for the rest of their lives. And as we build, it is up to each of us whether we have a building of which we can be proud.

Like most young children, my life wasn't too exciting the first few years. We spent all of our time with the family and within the household. Despite living under the same roof, we all developed our own individual personalities and interests. No two of us were (or are) alike.

Going to Sunday school with my sisters and brothers was a weekly event, regardless of the weather. It was there that I learned how God loves and protects us and that He will always be there when we need help. I found out later, however, that there is more to faith than that.

I remember the little red chairs and old-fashioned organ in the church basement, where the primary classes were held. We would sit in a circle, listen to Bible stories, and sing those memorable songs. I loved to hear the stories, and I tried to imagine how great God was and to understand that I could turn to Him in my times of need. At that age, I didn't have any real problems, so singing and praying came easy.

I guess you could have called us a middle-class family, or close to it, even if we didn't have electricity or indoor plumbing. The majority of families in our area were without those modern conveniences, too. We didn't miss them because we never had them. People don't miss what they've never had.

Our radio was a big floor model, and it sat in our living room. We used a car battery to power it, and when the battery went dead, we took it down to the gas station in town and had it charged. Dad always listened to the news; it was of great interest to him, as was reading the daily newspaper.

After the news, we listened to the other programs and used our imaginations. It was fun, not like today when all we have to do is sit in front of the television and watch pictures. During scary programs, our imaginations ran wild, and at times it was hard for me to go to sleep after listening to one such as Inner Sanctum.

We had no electricity, so we used kerosene lamps and lanterns. The cleaning of the lamp globes was a daily, dirty job. If they weren't scrubbed, they gave no light. It was hard enough to read with a clean globe, let alone a dirty one. The lanterns were also used outside for chores around the barn during the winter.

At the ripe old age of five, I loved to ride the little red, white, and blue school bus. There were three buses that served our school district; two went to Fordville and Hardwood. Since our town had the least amount of children, we got the little bus. It had a row of short seats down the center and a bench-like seat along each side. It held about thirty-five students. The other two buses were a lot bigger. Foster City, Fordville, and Hardwood made up our school district, which took in a rather large area in terms of miles.

That first year, my class consisted of about ten children. We got to know each other in just a few short weeks. We were mostly from the same kind of background, so we had much in common. Each town had its own nationality; ours was Swedish. The different nationalities didn't mix much, but, at that time, we didn't do much socializing any way.

The first year was routine. The kindergartners stayed all day at school, since the buses only ran in the mornings and afternoons. During the early afternoons, we took a nap on our trusty little rugs. In kindergarten, we learned to get along, and we played together and memorized some of the alphabet and a few numbers. But the best thing of all was the little town built of cardboard boxes that sat in the corner of the room. I enjoyed being the storekeeper best. We also had a post office and a gas station. We would pretend to shop in the store, put gas in our make-believe cars, and pick up the mail.

Then came spring, when the melting snow provided fast flowing streams and puddles, some of which were quite deep. Even if the water was cold, we would wade through every puddle we could fine. One time in particular, we waded through some puddles and were soaked to our waists. When we reached home, we kept our distance form Mom and Dad, but Mom sang, played the guitar, and told us stories we all loved. As we listened to one of her tales, I wanted to get closer to her. We always sat in a circle. I got too close and she felt my wet pants. She was very displeased with me, and I never heard the rest of her story. I was sent to my room, where I cried not only because I had missed the story, but because it bothered me that Mom was mad and I had disobeyed her. She was able to make me feel awful when I did something wrong, even if she didn't say much.

The summer went fast. Being only six years old, there wasn't much I could do in the way of chores, except pull a few weeds or so.

In the spring of 1943, when I was in second grade, I became better adjusted to school and to my classmates. I wasn't a very sociable person. I had started to play with the other children, but I still had no real friends. I didn't want anyone close to me. I was a loner, and I knew it was my own fault. Like anything else, people have to work at making friends. I loved taking the bus, and I thought that someday I would be a bus driver.

When I arrived home, I felt safe in my own world. I liked to play with our good old dog, Sally. I was able to talk to her, and she didn't laugh or run away. She would just sit as if she were listening to me every word.

We had a lot of cats on our farm. They kept the mouse population down, which was an ongoing battle. I often wondered if the cats ever got ahead of the situation.

The dogs were a big part of farm life. They helped with the cattle and saved us a lot of steps. They also protected the farm while we were away since we never locked anything. I don't even think we had keys for the buildings. Our first dog, Sally, came from Grandpa and Grandma. She was small with slick black fur. She had puppies every spring, and, of course, we couldn't keep them. Dad would have to give them away or have them put to sleep because we just couldn't keep six or seven puppies each spring.

The fall of my third year of school pretty much passed without fanfare, as it had the two years before. The holidays came and went, along with another Sunday school Christmas program, but as spring began to roll in, things changed. I wasn't prepared for the change, nor was anyone else.

It was on a spring day when Mom got sick. I suppose she hadn't felt well for months, but none of us kids knew about it. As we all know, parents try to keep unpleasant things from their children as long as they can, but things got worse, and Mom was taken to the hospital, Dad at her side. While in the hospital, she slipped into a coma. Her life was slipping away, but I knew God would make her well again because we needed her, and we all prayed in earnest for her recovery. I was taught that God was always near when we needed Him, and if we EVER needed Him, it was then. All we had to do was trust and believe, but things only got worse, and I couldn't understand why.

Mom passed away within a few weeks. She left six children and a husband who loved her very much and now had to go through life without her. We never quite got over the loss of my mother, even during the passing years.

Losing Mom at the age of seven was about all I could bear. I remember that dreadful day. Dad came home with tears in his eyes and told us that Mom had passed away to be with the Lord. He sat us down on the couch in the living room and tried to explain. I sat there in disbelief. I don't remember the words he used or how he said them, but in a few minutes his words sank in and my tears began to flow. He tried to comfort us.

I was glad I had a family like ours to lean on at that time, but I didn't understand why God had let that tragedy happen. Didn't He know that six children needed a mother? And why my family? I'd known other families that had lost loved ones through the years, but I wasn't interested in other families; I was interested in my family.

I started to blame God. I continued to attend Sunday school, but it wasn't the same for years. Now, as I look back, I thank God for my family, especially for Dad and the courage and love he gave us through the years. He became both mom and dad to us, and he had his hands full, but he didn't give up and leave us. He stayed with us when we needed him the most.

The funeral took place a few days after Mom died, and everyone in town came to pay their respects. Nearly every family had felt the loss of a loved one at one time or another; therefore, they felt compassion for our family. They understood what we were going through. They helped us with the chores, and the ladies provided food through the time of grief.

Then we were on our own, and that's when we really began to feel the loss. It was up to Dad whether we would stay together, be given to relatives, or put into foster homes. Some of our aunts and uncles wanted the older kids, but Walley and I weren't really wanted. Maybe it was our age. I remember hiding behind the couch in the living room, listening to the discussions. I sat there with tears in my eyes, feeling as if no one wanted me then or ever would. I felt so worthless. But Dad wouldn't let us be separated. He made the decision to keep us together, knowing full well what was in store for him. To this day, I will always love and respect him for making that choice so many years ago.

As I grew older, I couldn't thank God enough for giving us a father like Dad. He could have just walked out and let us go to foster homes, and the town folks wouldn't have thought any less of him for doing so. Instead, he stayed and set an example of what being a real Christian meant, not just with words, but with deeds. He had a lot of his mother in him.

After things settled into a regular routine, I still wasn't at ease with God. I still blamed him for our circumstances. There was no one to tuck us into bed or kiss us goodnight at the end of the day. Dad didn't have time after a long day's work, and in those days, fathers didn't do those things very often.

Since I was only seven years old when Mom passed away, I don't have as many memories of her as I do of Dad. He was the center of my world during the next few years, and as time went on, we all depended more and more on each other. We built a bond that lasted down through the years.

Grandma Swanson came and stayed with us for the summer, but she couldn't speak English, and we couldn't understand Swedish, so there were a lot of misunderstandings between us. We had what you might call a generation gap, but we always knew when she was angry, which wasn't very often. I guess it doesn't make any difference what language is used, when a person is angry, everyone knows it.

There was one trick we used to play on her when we didn't want to clean our rooms upstairs, and we didn't want her to check them. We would take the knob out of the upstairs door so she couldn't open it. This prank didn't happen often. Once she told Dad, it was a different story. Dad wasn't short on discipline. He didn't spare the rod. He ruled with a strong hand. There was no foolishness.

Grandma and Grandpa Swanson lived only four or five miles from us, so Dad saw them daily. Grandma no longer stayed with us, but she still baked and mended our clothes. She did a lot for us through the years.

I also enjoyed staying with her when it was just the two of us. She would read to me from the Bible and tell me stories about life when she was a little girl. I couldn't fully understand her because of the language barrier, but the way she spoke to me with her pleasant voice, I knew we understood each other. It's hard to explain, but I always felt at home with her.

I also enjoyed Grandpa Swanson, but in a different way. He was a rough-and-tough sort of person. He would let me ride the horses when he went to town or worked in the woods. He even taught Wally and me how to spit, and we got pretty good at it, too, until Grandma found out. Boy was mad at him for teaching us something like that, but we thought it was great.

The hardest thing was to go back to school that fall because the other kids had mothers. Things weren't the same anymore. Marion, the oldest, was now in charge of the household for the family, which was a very big load for such a small girl. She was only thirteen, and she had to take care of and help the rest of us. No one really gave her the credit she so deserved through those early years. She was a little girl one day and grown up the next, with all the responsibilities. She got the blame when things weren't done when Dad came home. If we didn't do our chores, she did them so she wouldn't get into trouble, and we took advantage of the situation. There were times I would catch her sitting on her bed and crying as if she had no one to help. How many thirteen-year-olds have had to help raise five sisters and brothers? But between all of us, we made it.

I had naturally curly hair, which was hard to control. Marion fixed it the best she could, but there wasn't much she could do with it. My second-grade teacher never thought my hair was fixed right, so she wouldn't leave me alone until she was able to recomb it. I don't know whether she felt sorry for me, or she was just nosy. She would take me into the back room, which was a little room that was sort of like a closet. The teachers kept their supplies and personal items there. Every morning when I arrived, she was waiting to do my hair.

When she combed it, it hurt! I was tender-headed, and the way she combed it made me cry. When I cried, she seemed to get rougher. I was afraid to tell Dad, and, of course, I would have never told Marion because she worked so hard to help me look good when I went to school. So, I just gritted my teeth and bore it the best I could. The worst thing was facing the other kids and listening to them tease me about the teacher having to comb my hair. It got to the paint that I would hide during recess and lunch hour. During lunch, I would take an extra-long time eating, and I even helped the cook clean up the lunchroom at times.

I knew it would be a long year with the school year starting out the way it did, but Grandma Omen came to my rescue. She took me to live with her in January, and I stayed with her the rest of the school year. What a blessing that arrangement was. Things picked up a bit for me, but I still missed my family, Grandma would tuck me in bed and kiss me good night before I went to sleep, and when she turned off the light in the little bedroom in which my mother had slept as a little girl, I had a real comfortable feeling. It was as if someone were sitting by the bed and watching over me.

Grandma and Grandpa did all they could to make me feel at home. Grandpa was always good for a few stories every night. When he came home from work, he would get out the old rocking horse my mom and her brothers had spent hours riding. It was worn, but that didn't make any difference to me. It was still fun to ride. He also read the funnies to me on Sunday mornings before I went to Sunday school. This experience was good therapy for me, even if it only lasted a few months. Mom's passing was also their loss; Mom was their only daughter.

I did well in school. The kids didn't know all that I had gone through, and I didn't tell anyone about my situation. At last, I had

33

children to play with who didn't tease me. I still lacked self-confidence, but I brought on a lot of my problems.

During the winter, the other children and I would slide on the road in front of Grandma's house. Few cars came that way. Grandma and Grandpa lived on a little farm with only a few cows, pigs, and chickens. It wasn't the same as the farm in Foster City. I remember the old tractor that sat out behind the barn and how we kids used to play on it. We made believe we were driving it. Grandma and Grandpa also had a dog. He was a little brown and white dog, and he even got to stay in the house at night. He slept in a little basket behind the cookstove in the kitchen. Since Grandpa worked in Iron Mountain at the Ford Motor Company, he didn't get home before six or so, so Grandma did the chores. It was fun helping her since we were never in a hurry. There wasn't much to do.

Once more, trouble came knocking at my door. I got lice from someone at school, and they were the nastiest things I had ever seen. They were hard to see, and the itching was terrible. Grandma went right to work on the problem, and she thought she had it whipped before I returned home when school was out for the summer.

When I arrived home, I was glad to be back no matter how good a time I'd had at Grandma's, but I didn't know I still had lice. So, the battle was on once again, because it didn't take long for the lice to spread to the whole family. This time, however, they were in six heads instead of just one.

It wasn't an easy task to get rid of them. We all had to get rid of them at the same time; otherwise, it was a waste of time. The treatment wasn't like it is today with all kinds of shampoos to take care of the problem. The only way to get rid of lice in those days was to kill them with kerosene. That's right! Kerosene! First of all, we had to cut our hair short, then we had to comb it with a fine-toothed comb to get most of the lice out, but that procedure still left the eggs to kill. Then came the kerosene treatment. We soaked our heads in it and wrapped our hair in towels for a few hours. Then we washed our hair over and over to get rid of the smell, which was better than the lice by a long shot. Sometimes we had to take the treatment three or four times to make sure we had gotten rid of them. By the start of the school year in the fall, we were clean once again, but thinking about the experience still makes my head itch. A lot of children had lice during those years.

It seemed to take such a long time to grow up. I just couldn't wait to be on my own because I thought all of my problems would be over with then. How wrong I was. I aged and started getting chores to do. It didn't take long before I, too, was doing my share of work on the farm. I could not wait until I could milk the cows and drive the horses. Housework never interested me, and I had my share of it. I just didn't like to cook, bake, and clean. I always wanted to work outside with the animals in the fields.

In early spring, the farmers made ready for planting. There was a lot to do. The fields had to be plowed and prepared for seeding. We cut the seed potatoes, a task that was done by hand and at night after our chores were finished. We treated the corn seeds so the crows wouldn't eat them before they had a chance to take root and grow. If we didn't treat them, the crows would follow us down the rows and eat the kernels as fast as we planted them. It was an ongoing battle to keep ahead of the birds.

Preparing the garden was an important part of our lives. First, we planted the grain and potatoes, and as the soil became warmer, we planted the corn. Dad could always tell when to plant by the moon and the stars, and he could foresee the weather. Knowing when to plant was very important to the farmers, whose lives consisted of good weather and prayer, mostly prayer.

In the spring, when the snow melted and the fresh, green grass and wildflowers sprouted into full bloom, I loved to wander through the woods and pick the different flowers. I didn't know many of their names, but that didn't matter. One of the prettiest was the wild Lilly. I could see why God spoke of them in the Bible. As I sat and looked at the wildflowers, it seemed a small voice said to me, "Enjoy

God's beauty. God is still in charge of the things in this world." I started to understand God better, but I wasn't ready to completely trust Him. Praying came more easily as time went along. Thank God He never gave up on me, or the rest of the world for that matter.

Every spring, Sally had a litter of puppies, and we each picked one out as our own, knowing we couldn't keep them. But one year, Anna picked out a black-and-white puppy and with her help, Micky survived for sixteen years or more. He became a very important part of our lives.

In May, we let the cows out during the day to eat the fresh spring grass, which was sweet and tender after a long winter of dry hay: and a real treat for them. Wild leeks, from the onion family, grew along with the fresh grass and wildflowers, and the cows always seemed to find them and eat them, too. The leeks would go through their systems and we could taste them in the milk. Thank God that entrée only lasted a few weeks because when the taste or smell of the leeks was too strong, we couldn't sell the milk. During that time of year, I passed up drinking milk. Try putting onions in your milk, and you will experience the taste I am talking about.

After the spring planting was over, the summer life began. The month of May came to a close, and school was shut down for another summer. On Memorial Day, we honored the men and women who so bravely gave of themselves so we might remain free. We take this blessing for granted, and we shouldn't lose sight of our country's freedoms and values and the people who preserved them through the years. If we were to spend some time in another country, we would appreciate good old America.

To get ready for Memorial Day services, we cleaned up the cemetery. We cut the grass, pulled the weeds, and cleared away the leaves and debris that had accumulated through the winter. We took a lot of pride in our cemetery. The whole family took part in the cleaning, which took us a day or two. We also cleaned the lots of those people whose families had moved out of the area. When the cleanup was finished and the flowers planted, which would last until the first frost, we were ready for Memorial Day services.

I always looked forward to Memorial Day. I had a certain feeling as I stood by the road watching the soldiers march by in full-dress uniforms. They looked so sharp. Some had outgrown their uniforms a little, but the spirit was still there, and that's what made the difference. As the soldiers marched, I got goose bumps. The spectacle made me feel ten feet tall, and I thought about how great it must be to be in the service. I didn't realize what I was dreaming about because war isn't pleasant, and no one ever wins. How lucky the soldiers were to have come back alive. Others' lives had been cut down in the prime of life. An American flag was placed on each soldier's grave, then the minister took a moment to honor those who had given their lives so that we might be free. The Memorial Day services also included a social gathering of sorts.

By late afternoon, as the events of the day came to a close, we turned our attention to the top of the hill. As the sun was about to go down, a soldier stood, bugle in hand, and played Taps with great pride. We all stood at attention. We didn't have to be told to do so. The response came automatically, even for the children.

We were all united, even if only for a moment.

As I continued to attend Memorial Day services in different areas, I often thought back to the days in Foster City when we remembered our fallen comrades. Since then, we have gone through more wars, and each generation has done its part to keep America free. It's great to be in a country that has always been able to rise to the occasion when needed.

After Memorial Day, school was out, and the real farm work began. It seemed we just didn't have enough time for ourselves. The days weren't long enough. Summer was nearing. We had to care for the cows, the horses, and the rest of the animals.

In the fall, the crops had to be harvested and preserved for another winter. We raised chickens for eggs and meat, and we had to fatten up the pigs for butchering.

When the spring snow melted, it left ponds of water in the low areas. We built rafts and pretended we were Tom Sawyer. We nailed a few boards together and found long sticks to push ourselves around a pond. Sometimes the rafts didn't float very well, and we would find ourselves at the bottom of a pond. Thank God the ponds weren't very deep. Sometimes we would find ourselves shipwrecked along the creek bank. It seemed we were always wet, but it was a lot warmer, nearly summer.

One little fellow we found hanging around the pond was the frog. We heard from him in early spring and summer. The frogs told us that spring had arrived, and summer was just around the corner. The frogs' voices were like music to my ears. I loved to lay in bed at night and listen to them. To most people, their croaking was just noise, but not to me. The scene was being set for another busy summer, a time to which I looked forward.

Chapter Three
Summer on the Farm

I had been telling my daughters about life on the farm, and they wondered what we did for a pastime. I must say we spent most of our time working. It's good that we remember most of the good times and are able to forget the not-so-good times. We had a lot of those. I also tried to tell my daughters about my experiences in a way they would understand. Life is so different for us now. The biggest difference is the fact that they don't live on a farm. Life is so different growing up in town.

Late May and early June was the popple season. It lasted only a month or so. While sap is returning to a tree's trunk, the tree's bark comes off easily. We had to cut and peal as many trees as possible during this time. The whole family pitched in and put in some long days. Dad and Johnny cut and trimmed the trees, and the rest of us peeled off the bark. We had to do a little of everything to make ends meet, and this activity was one of those things.

After we peeled the logs and while they were still wet and sticky from the sap, we would sit on a piece of bark and slide down them. If there were a knot sticking up on a log, there was no way to stop, so we took our chances. I scratched my legs more than once, but the experience didn't stop me from participating in that sport year after year.

Between popple season and haying, we did chores such as weeding the garden and picking berries. We did whatever had to be done. It seemed there was no break in sight, and we all had a lot to do.

We had to make our own entertainment. We could climb to the top of a tree and swing from a slim tree to the ground, and we had fun doing such things, which is what it was all about.

I enjoyed working with the horses. They were a big part of farm life during those early years, unlike today when tractors do the work. There was just something about horses doing the work.

In between harvesting the crops, we logged. Both farming and logging were done as a family. While we worked in the woods, I enjoyed lunchtime most of all. We always ate a few sandwiches and drank Kool-Aid while Dad drank his coffee. After lunch, we would all sit around and talk or just lie under a tree and take a nap. Before I was old enough to work in the woods, it was my job to take the lunch to Dad and Johnny.

As I walked through the woods, I loved to watch the birds or maybe a wild animal or two. The birds always seemed so busy, and the deer were beautiful and graceful. Since I knew I had better not be late with the lunches, I took the long way home. I enjoyed being by myself at times like that.

During logging, we seldom drove the horses into the woods. One person was at the landing, and he would cut and stack the logs. The horses were sent up to the person in the woods, and they would be hooked up to the load of logs and sent back to the landing. Later, we would haul the logs to the rail-road spur and ship them to the mill. Now and then, we had a horse that would not work. It would want to go home instead of to the woods, and it would just make a detour around the landing and head for the barn, logs and all. If a log caught on anything, the horse just kept going. Sometimes a harness would be torn, and we would have to go home and fix it before bringing the horse back to finish the day. Each horse was different. Like people, horses have a mind of their own.

We always had a big garden. It was hard to keep ahead of the weeds. I had the pleasure of pulling them and thinning the onions, carrots, and lettuce when those plants were up about two or three inches. I was the youngest girl, and taking care of the garden was one of my chores. It seemed to last forever.

During one of the many times, I grew tired of pulling weeds, I decided I would cultivate the garden and get rid of the weeds once and for all. I figured it wouldn't take long to get the job done. At the same time, I would have fun doing it for a change, but I needed help, so I convinced my sister to help me. I thought I was pretty smart thinking up the idea.

I harnessed up old Red and hooked him to a cultivator, which took an hour. If we had been weeding during that time, we would have had most of it done, but my way was better, I thought. The horse was hard enough to handle and trying to cultivate between the narrow rows of the garden was impossible. The horse stepped on the weeds, along with the vegetables. The garden wasn't like the corn or potato fields where the rows were planted to allow the cultivator. We dug up the weeds all right, but the vegetables came up, too. We quickly replanted them and threw away the weeds. That afternoon, the garden looked great, but by the next day, in the summer heat and with the lack of rain, the vegetables did not take root and before long they were all dried up.

Once again, I was in trouble. I just knew there would be another trip to the woodshed. It had been my idea. It was my fault, and, of course, the one thing I knew better than to do was lie. If I did, and Dad found out, it would make the punishment worse. Once again, I took my punishment. I didn't have much choice. We didn't raise a garden for fun. We planted it for fresh vegetables through the summer and to store the remaining crops for the upcoming winter. Dad did not believe in wasting a summer's work on a dumb idea like mine. I had to plant new seeds and restart the garden. It didn't turn out too well that year, but at least we got a few things out of it that summer.

I believe I made more trips to the woodshed than the rest of my sisters and brothers, at least it seemed that way to me. I'm not saying I did not deserve it; but I am saying my ideas weren't the best at times.

The month of July was one of the driest of the year, and it was haying season. At that time, we put in a lot of long days, and we were tired by the time the weekend came along.

During the week, we had to catch the horses each morning. We would ger a bucket of oats and shake it, but as summer passed, we ran out of oats, so we substituted sand for grain. When we shook the bucket, it sounded the same. The horses would hear it, and thinking we had oats, they would come right to us. Once they found out we didn't have oats in the bucket, we had but one chance to get a rope around their necks. If we missed, it was too late. Instead, we would have to chase them into the barn, and that was a lot harder. It didn't take long for the horses to figure us out, so we ended up keeping them in the barn at night, which was a lot easier on us.

Like I said before, kids in those days made their own entertainment. It was not like today, when we all think the cities and towns in which we live should provide it for us and our children. Back on the farm, we did the best we could with last-minute notice, and much of the time, our ideas weren't the greatest.

Sunday was our only day off. We did the regular chores and went to Sunday school, but other than that, we had the rest of the day to ourselves. Dad would visit Grandma and Grandpa Swanson every Sunday afternoon, just like clockwork. So, we were on our own then. Many times, we would ride the horses, the same horses that worked all week. With us around, they didn't even have one day off. We would take the clock from the kitchen, put it on a fence post, and ride by every so often to check on the time. None of us had a watch, so this procedure was the next best thing. We always knew when Dad was coming home;

we could see him driving down the road long before he got to our road and started up the hill. We always took turns on lookout so that by the time he got to the top of the hill, we were all back doing the things we should have been doing, and everything looked normal.

We never had saddles; we always rode bareback. The horses we rode were work horses. We never had fancy riding horses. Dad had access to a lot of horses through the summer. The horses were left by the local cattle dealer. Dad used the horses in return for the cattle dealer's use of the pasture for his horses. Some of the animals were crazy. We took our chances when we jumped on their backs, and sometimes it was a bit too late. All we could do was hang on. A few times, the trips were real short. Riding bareback, we didn't have much to hang onto except the mane. Thank God Dad never cut their manes.

On one particular day, Wally and I went riding. I chose a pretty, black horse, but that was all that went in my favor. The horse was fast all right, but he also had a mind of his own. Once I was on his back, it was too late to change my mind, even had I wanted. Once he got going, I wasn't able to control him.

We used oats to catch the horses. We poured the oats on the ground, and while the horses were eating, we put on the bridle and jumped on their backs. Once they were through eating, we had better be ready.

As we passed, the horse noticed a kernel or two, and to my surprise, he decided he wanted to check it out by making a ninety-degree turn. I wasn't ready for it, and I didn't make a turn with him. I just went straight ahead, right into a brush pile. Boy was I a mess! My arms were all scratched and bruised. I was able to move them, so Wally and I figured they weren't bro-ken. I know this method wasn't the best way to check them, but it was the best we could do. Nowadays, I would have gone to a doctor, but not back then. For one thing, we weren't supposed to be riding the horses in the first place, so we had to take our chances.

My arms looked bad, but we couldn't tell Dad because we weren't supposed to be riding the horses. As the days passed, my arms looked worse before they looked better. I wore a long sleeve shirt in the middle of summer to cover my arms. It was very hot, which made me feel worse. It seemed as if it took forever for my arms to heal so that I could put away that shirt. If Dad had found out, he would have been furious, and he would have had a right to be.

Another fun thing we did when Dad was gone was to send our trusty dog, Micky, out to greet anyone who came to the house, especially if it were a salesman. When Micky got to the car, he would growl and show a tooth or two. He had a great talent for looking vicious, but he never bit anyone. No one knew that, though. Nobody had the nerve to get out of the car and test Micky. I don't think I would have either had I been one of those people. Micky would do anything we told him to, even if we weren't using our better judgment, and it was fun to hide and watch Micky in action.

Another chore of mine was going to get the cows. Sometimes it was hard to find them. They were able to graze on about sixty acres, and that's a lot of territory to cover when most of it is covered with trees, except for a few clearings here and there, and especially when I was looking for twenty or thirty heads of cattle. We didn't have horses for that job. We had to walk everywhere.

It was hard when it was raining because they would stay under cover. They didn't move much on hot days either. They just lay in the shade. One cow had a bell, and the rest followed her. If I couldn't hear the bell, I would have to guess where I thought they might be and hope I was right. At times, I wasn't very lucky. If I didn't find them right away, I had to stay out until I did. Dad wasn't much on excuses. Anytime he went out to find the cows, he found them. It didn't make any difference whether it was raining or in the heat of the day. He seemed to find them immediately, anywhere, anytime.

There was also another reason for my being late at times. As the summer came and the rains were far and few between, the creek started to dry up. It was spring fed, so there was always a little water flowing, but by the middle of summer it was mostly mud, and I mean mud, a foot or so deep at least. When it was hot, it was fun to sit for a few minutes and soak my feet in the creek. I would end up lying in the creek and getting completely soaked. By the time I decided to be on my way it would have been too late, but it felt good, and I would dry off long before I got home.

During the summer, I went barefoot a lot. It was so nice to play on the grass and the mud down by the creek. The cows thought so, too, because they crossed the creek and stood in the mud to cool off. By the time they got home, the mud would be dried, and what a mess it was to clean them up for milking. We used a lot of soap and water. As soon as they were wet the mud just ran off them, and a mud puddle would form under each cow by the time we were finished.

One day while I was playing in the mud on my way home with the cows, I stepped on a stick, and it stuck in the bottom of my foot. I sat on a stump to pull it out, but a piece of it remained in my foot. I thought I had removed it all and the pain would go away in a few days. As the days passed, I began to limp, and my foot became infected. Dad wanted to know what was wrong. At first, I tried to hide it, but one day he checked the foot. He took out his trusty pocketknife and dug out the silver. It wasn't too deep, but the procedure didn't help the pain any.

Nurse Carison was always called in when things were too serious for us to handle ourselves, but this was one of those times Dad took care of it. He got out the bottle of iodine, which was used to kill infection, and that hurt worse. After a few days, the foot was fine, thanks to Dad; otherwise, I could have gotten blood poisoning and no telling what else. In those days, however, all I thought about was the pain and not about what could have happened in the future.

Once again, Wally and I had a great idea, which was to catch animals and bring them home so we could take them and keep them for pets. Through the years, we caught all sorts of small animals and birds. One day we found a baby crow on the ground. It had fallen out of the nest. It was okay, but it was scared and hungry. We brought it home, put it in a cage, and fed it chicken feed. It wasn't long before it was ready to go back to the wild, and on Dad's request, we let it go. Dad's requests were usually orders.

We also found a woodchuck. We really didn't find him in trouble. He was doing fine on his own, but we wanted to take him home, so we knocked him out with a rock and put him in our lunch pail. We brought him home and put him in a cage, but when he came to, he was furious and tried to get out. We intended to tame him whether he liked it or not. The first thing I thought about was putting my hand in the cage to pet him, which turned out to be a big mistake. Even being in the cage, he was still wild. We all know what happened next. He bit my finger, and for weeks I walked around knowing I was going to die of rabies, but that fate didn't come to pass either. It seemed I had learned my lesson the hard way, a trend that wasn't about to change in the near future.

I always took Micky with me whenever I went anywhere, especially when it was dark. You hear or think you see things that aren't really there, which can be scary when you are alone. I knew Micky could handle anything or anyone that came our way.

Our kerosene lamps, which gave off long shadows, were scary in themselves, and listening to frightening programs on the radio didn't help either. When we went to sleep at night, we didn't have a night-light. We went to sleep in the dark, and I mean DARK! a lot of nights I would lay in bed and see things in the dark. Then I would cover my head with a blanket and try to sleep, but rest came hard on many nights.

One day, when Micky and I went to get the cows, I was walking along and talking to him. Like his mother, Sally, he seemed to listen. Of course, he never spoke back or argued with me. Then I looked up and saw a big, black bear! It seemed as if he were so close I could have reached out and touched him. He was eating berries and wasn't interested in Micky or me, but I didn't waste any time checking him out more closely. We just took the long way around to get the cows. Of course, out there by myself, all kinds of crazy thoughts ran through my mind, including the bear chasing me or killing me. Bears had killed people who got in their way, but that fate was rare.

Once I found the cows, they went right by the bear. Neither the bear nor the cows went out of their way, but I did. I took the long way around, and I walked the rest of the way home with one eye looking over my shoulder. Despite the experience, I still enjoyed going after the cows, even when I really had no choice. I always enjoyed watching the little animals scamper about and seeing the bird's fly overhead, and, or course, throughout the summer, I could also watch the deer run around.

One little varmint we avoided was a skunk. Skunks have a smell all their own, and it seemed that our dogs were always attracted to them and came out on the short end of the deal. One day, Micky came into contact with one of those little fellows, and he, too, came out on the short end. Wally and I felt sorry for him and tried to help. We decided to wash him, but as soon as the water hit his coat, it made the smell worse. We, along with Micky, could not stand the smell, but he had to live with it. It took two or three weeks for the smell to wear off and wetting his coat hadn't helped. It only made the smell worse. Later I found out that if we had used tomatoes, the acid would have helped relieve the smell. We never washed Micky again.

During the summer when I was ten or eleven years old, I wanted to learn how to milk the cows, and Dad finally said okay. I was so thrilled, but little did I know this request would lead to a full-time job in the future. Through the years, I was glad I had learned because I loved working outside. Milking was one job we all did, and since we milked the cows by hand, the more hands we had the better. Along with milking the cows, I was also doing more and more farm work.

Still, I felt I could never be as good as Anna and Johnny, and for sure, I could not be like Marion. As far as I was concerned, Marion was the greatest. For one thing, Anna, Johnny, and Marion never seemed to get into trouble like I did. Dad would tell me how good they did things compared to me. After a while, I thought I would never get up to their level, but I'm sure Anna, Johnny, and Marion felt the same at one time or another. Marion was such comfort. She really tried to take Mom's place when it came to listening to my little problems. She had plenty of her own problems, but she still had time for me. Most of all, she taught me how to pray, which she knew how to do better than most. It was something she gave me, and no one could take it away. Prayer is a learning process, just like the other things we learn to do throughout our lives, and we must practice it. The more we practice praying, the better we get at it, and our faith increases.

One of the biggest problems in the summer was flies. They were plentiful. We were forever spraying to get rid of them. We sprayed the house daily. We had screens on the doors and windows, but they seemed to come and go as they pleased. Before we could spray in the house, we had to cover everything because the solution was so strong.

When it came to the cattle in the barn, the situation was a lot worse. Here again, killing flies was an ongoing battle. It seemed as if for every fly we killed, two took its place. It was like an army, and we were enemies. We had to spray morning and night, and the evenings were the worst. The flies waited all day for the cows to come home.

As we milked them, the cows were forever hitting us with their tails, and we continuously swatted the flies. We had to tie the cows' tails to one of their hind legs. When milking a cow by hand, it's hard enough to balance on the little stool and hold the pail between your legs without the cow's tail hitting you in the face, too.

Then came the trusty old horsefly, which bit hard enough to draw blood. We would put a piece of burlap over the horses' noses while they worked so the flies could not bite them, but once in a while the flies' bit through the protection. Horseflies were a lot harder to kill, I guess because they are a lot big-ger and healthier than little, old houseflies. Killing flies was a battle all summer long, and it was a relief when the cold weather came and killed them.

We had a lot to do when the haying season approached. Cutting and gathering hay was one of the hardest jobs on the farm. The speed of the sickle depended on the speed of the mower, and the horses had to keep up a good pace, especially when the grass was thick. After the hay was cut, it had to lay and dry for three or four days.

We also used the horses to rake the hay into windrows, then we stacked it. I drove horses during hay season because it was the easiest job. While Dad and Johnny loaded the wagon, I drove and packed the hay on the wagon. The better it was packed, the easier it was to unload. It was a real challenge for me, and it was a time when I wasn't compared to my brothers and sisters.

Once the bay was in the barn, we used a big fork to unload the wagon. The fork ran on a track. Now and then, we got the horses going too fast and couldn't stop them in time. We would pull the fork and all through the other end of the barn, and another repair job was in order.

The younger kids, Ruthie, Wally, and I, had to crawl up into the hayloft to pack the hay so we could get as much of it in as possible. I would think about the snakes that might be in the hay, and I couldn't wait to get out and do something else.

We used to kill snakes out in the fields and hang them on the back of the wagon. When I was a kid, I thought if you cut a snake in half, it would grow back together when the sun went down. Of course, that feat is impossible. It, too, was just a myth.

When people moved into a new area, they put pugs in the area first to get rid of the snakes. The pigs drove the snakes out or killed them.

We couldn't do any haying when the dew was on the ground. So, every morning, for the first few hours, we waited for the sun to dry the hay, and we picked raspberries. We picked at least two hundred quarts of raspberries each summer for the coming winter, along with the raspberries we ate during berry season. I dreaded picking the berries even if I did like to eat them. Ruthie, Wally, and I did the picking, and Anna and Marion got to can of the berries.

Once we picked the berries, we had to wash the cans when we got home, which gave me an idea for finishing faster. I decided to put a few leaves in the bottom of my pail, but later I became braver and braver, and I put in more and more leaves. One day, that trick came to a halt. Dad was sitting at the table, and he decided to help me clean my berries. You can guess the rest. To correct the problem, I had to pick an extra pailful of raspberries each morning to make up for the shortage. I didn't put leaves in my pail ever again.

One day while Wally and I were picking berries, we found a bees' nest, and, of course, we couldn't keep away from it. The bees would not have bothered us if we had left them alone, but we just couldn't do that. We found a board, thinking that if we hit it directly, we could destroy it with one blow. Knowing full well we had only one chance, we smacked the nest. I have never seen so many mad bees, and I mean they were mad! We headed for home,

the bees close behind, and the rest is history. It was lucky we weren't allergic to hee stings, or we would still be suffering today.

After the haying season came to a close in July and August, the fields began drying up. We let the cattle graze in the hay fields as the second crop started to grow again. They really liked the new, tender grass. We had to watch them every evening to make sure they didn't get into the crops that had not been harvested. They ate continually as summer rolled onward, and finally, electric fences came into being.

The electric fences ran off of batteries, and we connected chargers. We put up short, wooden posters with little white insulators and a single wire. We had to move the fences quite often, so the simpler they were put up, the better They did the job, at least most of the time. The electric shock didn't seem to bother some cows, and they continually went through the fences. It didn't take us long to figure out we could have fun with the electric fences, too.

We would put a pail on the fence. Animals, especially horses, were very inquisitive. They would check out the pail and get a shock, but some never gave up. They would investigate the pail every time. Of course we had a good laugh, but now that I look back, it wasn't funny.

50

We knew the shock wasn't very strong since the fence ran on batteries. Then we decided to hook up some other fences.

The yard fence was a good place to start, along with the front, metal gate. When someone came to the house, he or she would touch the front gate handle. We would turn on the juice and watch the person jump back wondering what was going on. Then, when Dad went out to greet the visitor, we turned off the electricity. He could never understand why the people. acted as they did. When he opened the gate, nothing happened, and no one said anything. The visitors just felt foolish, I guess. This prank went of for some time, but like everything else, we got careless and wired up everything we could. One day, Dad opened the granary door while the electricity was on, and he was shocked, to say the least. It was no longer a laughing matter. He made me open the door with the electricity on. The door had a metal latch, and it was hard to open. I don't know whether it was the shock itself or just knowing that the electricity was on, but I finally opened the door, dancing around without music. That episode, of course, was the end of that game as far as I was concerned. Once again, I had paid the price for doing something I wasn't supposed to, and I wasn't the only one who did it. We were all in on the mischief. It usually took one or two of us to think up great ideas.

We had a lot of chickens on the farm, and they were such a mess. They were always hungry. We couldn't walk by the chicken coop without them following us. It didn't matter if they had just been fed or not. They still ran after us. We penned them up the best we could, but there were always chickens who found a way out. It didn't seem to matter how good the fences were. They found a hole or flew over. In order to stop their escapes, we clipped one

of their wings so they couldn't keep their balance. Wing clipping was a time-consuming chore, since we had to clip the wings of at least a hundred or more chickens.

Every spring, we received a lot of baby chicks through the mail. They were always a few days old. We put them behind the kitchen stove to keep them warm. After a few weeks they were strong enough to join the other chickens in the coop. We used an old wood stove in the center of the coop, and we had to take turns keeping the fire going all night. We raised a couple hundred chickens each year. Most were hens, but now and then we had a few roosters.

I remember one red rooster in particular. He was mean from the start. We began to tease him, and one day he got out of his pen and caught Wally in the backside. He only hurt Wally's pride, but I think having our pride hurt while we were growing up was worse than if we were hurt otherwise.

The pigs were a different story. They were a lot cleaner than the chickens and less noisy. All they wanted was their mud hole in the corner of the pen and something to eat. The files didn't bother them much either. They couldn't penetrate their thick skin.

One day, Dad had us clean the basement. We found a shelf with a few jars of apple juice that had fermented. We got the idea to mix it in the pig feed. The pigs loved it, and before we knew it, they were drunk. They acted much like people do when they drink. Some of the animals got mean, but they all acted differently. Once again, we all had a good laugh, and we couldn't pass up the chickens. They acted crazy, too. The roosters tried to crow in the middle of the day.

One summer, we had a runt pig. He was the craziest pig ever. He kept getting out of his pen and going in with the cows in the pasture. He kept climbing out of his pen, and we continued to add boards until the side of his pen was five or six feet high, but he still climbed over. We finally gave up and let him in with the cows. He never missed a day and went through the mud and the creek. He was always on the run, and being so small, it was hard for him to keep up with the cows. He wasn't like the other pigs, who lay around and grew fat. I guess that's why he stayed so thin. He knew he wasn't worth butchering, and he became a family pet.

One summer, between haying and butchering, Wally and I spend a few weeks with Grandma and Grandpa Omen. It was nice to stay with them. I was just one of six children, and being second to the youngest, it seemed I got lost in the shuffle. Being at Grandma's was different. She had time for us. She made us feel like we were somebody. When people came to the house for a visit, they always made comments about how well Marion, Johnny, and Anna were doing or what they had accomplished. Grandma had a way of making us feel important, at least she did with me. She always appreciated the things we did for her, which, at our age, wasn't much. She always had a treat for us. Now that I am a grandma, I know that's what grandmas do, spoil their grandchildren once in a while.

The day we hurt her feelings is one day I will never forget. One day when we had nothing to do, I dared Wally to cut down her flowers by the pump house. She always had beautiful flowers, and she was proud of them. Wally took the sickle and cut them down, and, oh, how funny we thought it was! I knew Wally would get into trouble, but it didn't work out that way. She saw what we had done, and she was so disappointed in us. She knew Wally and I cut them and that I had had a part in it. I wish she would have spanked us or something, but she didn't. I remember the look on her face and how we tried to make it up to her. We did anything she asked, and then some, but there wasn't much we could do, and that made it worse. Thank God she for-gave us, and we loved her all the more for it. I am glad, also, that God is so forgiving and doesn't give up on us, or I would have been lost long ago.

The one thing we loved to do was to take Grandma's cows to pasture, which was about two miles from the farm. Grandma always made things fun to do. We picked berries along the way and flowers on our way home. Sometimes we stopped and visited neighbors and ended up with some treat or another. Grandma's neighbors always had a lot of goodies. Visiting her was fun. There was always plenty of time to do things. It wasn't like back home where there was so much to do in so little time. In no time, our visit came to an end, and we were back home. Once again, we were glad to be home. It's like that in life. Even if our home isn't the best, it's still the best place to be.

When we returned home, it was time to harvest the grain. Dad would cut it with a binder that was drawn by a team of horses. The binder would cut and tie the grain into bundles, and we shocked six or eight bundles together. If we didn't shock the bundles right, they would fall over with the first wind or rain, and we would have to do the job over. On the farm, we never wanted to do a job a second time. We had to let the grain dry out, stack it, and get ready for the thresher crews. All the farmers had to take turns, since there was only one machine in Foster City.

Other pests we had on the farm were the deer. A lot of people did not consider them pests, but we did when we found them in our grain fields. They could destroy a field overnight because they came in herds of hundreds or more to feed in the cool of the evening. We took pot shots at them with a 22-caliber rifle to scare them out of the fields, and now and then we shot one for meat, even if they weren't in season. Deer was our only source of fresh meat in the summer, and it tasted great. It was a good change from the canned meat we were used to eating. Most families killed the deer year-round and used the meat to feed their families. Deer was the only meat many of us had and we never wasted it.

Then it was our turn for the threshing crew. All the farmers would get together and help each other. Only one man in town owned and operated the machine, and he would go around to all the farms in the area and thresh the grain. The crew went from farm to farm, and the job took the biggest part of August. Each farm had one or more men on the crew. Dad and Johnny went to our farm. When the crew came to our farm, we had to feed the men, and there were up to ten or twelve men on the crew. Each farm family served the best meal possible, and we were no different, except that we girls prepared it. Marion and Anna were in charge of the meal, and Ruthie and I helped when needed. Marion and Anna baked pies and prepared other food. I got stuck with the jobs of setting the table, washing the dishes, and cleaning up afterward. We always provided lemonade that was made with real lemons, most of the time. We squeezed lemons and oranges and put the juice from both in our lemonade.

I liked the summer even if we did work the hardest during that time of the year. Most rewarding was that we accomplished a lot in a few short months. I learned a lot about myself through hard work. We knew when something had to be done, and we got it done. Such lessons aren't learned in books.

We never went camping, as my husband and I have done with our daughters. Living in the country, I suppose there wasn't much need or time for it. The closest we ever got to camping was setting up a tent in the backyard. We tied a rope from one apple tree to another and put a piece of canvas or a blanket over it. That was our tent. We tried to sleep out there at night, but we didn't last more than a few hours. The ground was cold and damp even in the summer. It was cold at night, and we felt much better in our beds. Once the sun went down, it didn't take long to cool off; otherwise, it would be so hot at night it would be hard to sleep. It seemed to be one extreme or the other, and we never seemed to strike a happy medium.

Once again, it was time to move on, and in no time, we were back in school. Farm work slowed a little, and we went back to our books.

Chapter Four
Fall on the Farm

Once the fair was over, life went back to normal. Fall set in, and we went back to school for another year. It was always nice to start the school year with new clothes, but by spring we looked pretty ratty. It was nice to show off the new things we had acquired during the summer and to tell our friends about our experiences over the summer. Of course, we all tried to outdo each other when it came to telling stories, like all kids do.

We made the most of our school clothes. We had all learned to sew on an old treadle sewing machine, which was a lot easier than sewing by hand. My troubles were still with me, however, because it took me a lot longer to make a dress than it did my sisters. By the time I was finished with it, it already looked old. Most of the time one of my sisters ended up helping me with it, but then, I didn't care for that sort of thing. It had to be done, though, and I knew it! I believe that was one of the reasons I had so much trouble getting it done. I didn't contribute a lot of effort. We made many blouses from flour sacks, and we had five or six different patterns. Thank God we didn't have to make our coats and such. I would have frozen to death!

Even with school in session, the chores remained our top priority. We did them in the morning before leaving for school and again in the evening after school, and the colder the weather, the more there was to be. Because of our chores, we weren't able to take part in after-school activities. Most of the farm kids were in the same boat. Anyone who has ever lived on a farm knows there's always something to do, regardless of the time or season, and we were no different.

Every evening, Wally and I had to carry in the wood and water for the next day. We had to fill a big wood box behind the stove. There was a tank for water on the side of the stove, which kept the water hot.

We had to fight, though, before we began our chores. The winner got to pick which job he or she wanted. The fight took more time than the chores did. It didn't make much sense, except for the fact that we got pretty good at fighting. We were at the age where we were fairly well matched, but as we grew older, Wally got stronger, and in later years I was no match for him.

When Dad caught us fighting, we went to the woodshed. One would think we would have learned our lesson, but we were both stubborn, and it took a lot to get our attention, you might say.

We had to ride the bus to school. That was a lot of fun, too, except for the times I got kicked off for horsing around. In those days, the driver had only to stop the bus and put us off. It didn't matter where we were on the route. We just got off and started walking, either home or to school. In the morning, if we arrived late at school, there was no excuse. The teacher would already know why we were late, and it was best just to keep our mouths shut and take our punishment. There were times when I wanted to say something, but I knew better. In those days, kids were never right, and if we were, we were afraid to stand up and argue. We were never asked for our side of the story. As an adult, I, too, spent years as a bus driver, and the experience brought back memories of my childhood.

Now, if I were kicked off the bus on the way home, it was a different story. Coming home late from school meant I had to face Dad, and he didn't make deals either. Of course, it was my fault for staying in trouble continuously.

Another thing we didn't do was destroy the books from the school because they belonged to the school, not to us. We didn't even destroy our own things deliberately, because we only got one notebook each fall, and we had to make it last all year. By spring, our notebooks would hardly stay together.

Our teachers had authority, which is a concept that has changed in today's world. There is much about this new philosophy that I think is very wrong. The teacher has to have authority in order to do his or her job. As I look back on my education, the teachers who were the strictest were the best. We learned from them, and what we learned stayed with us down through the years. A teacher helps to mold a child's life, whether good or bad.

One of my greatest fears was flunking school, which was exactly what happened if a student didn't make the grades. There was no feeling sorry for the student who spent the next year in the same grade with a new group of students. Everyone knew why he or she was there. Thank God that was one setback I managed to escape. I was an average student, nothing to brag about.

One thing I hated was when Dad handed me the newspaper and asked me read aloud to him. Even if I knew the word, I sometimes hesitated a bit to make sure, which didn't help any. The longer I looked at the word, the more unsure I became. When I read, Dad did something else, but he still listened, and if I made a mistake, he knew. Sometimes he made me spell, and spelling was a subject that gave me a lot of trouble. These sessions really helped me, however, even if I didn't want to participate at the time.

By the way, students never got too big for the teacher. I just know the early teachers knew karate and self-defense techniques because they handled any and every situation. It didn't make a difference whether the student was male or female, big or small. Kids were just better off not trying anything. Of course, there were kids who tried to bend the rules, but to their surprise, the teachers were always victorious. They let everyone know who was in charge, and no one ever fought the system. I had some teachers who took advantage of the fact that the student was always wrong, but most of our teachers were great, and we learned from them. The one exception was the teacher who combed my hair every day and made me feel inferior.

When kids got into trouble in school, the teachers would contact their parents and have them come to the school to take care of the problem. Most people didn't have phones, so the parents would have to go to the school in person. Some families lived twenty to thirty miles away, so a summons had to be about an important issue. In my situation, Dad came to the school at any time of the day because he was on the school board all the years I went through school in Foster City. He had first-hand information on all the events, and so if and when I got into trouble, I took whatever punishment I might have coming. I found out in a hurry to keep my mouth shut.

I always liked to listen to our grandparents' stories of how hard they had it compared to us, how they had to walk ten miles or more to school, uphill both ways. We hung on their every word. I can't say we had to walk a long way. We only had to walk the hill to catch the bus. In the winter, when it was below zero, that was far enough. Micky, our good old trusty dog would walk with us. In the morning, when the bus came, he would lie in front of the bus until we got on, then he would go back home until evening. After school he would be at the bottom of the hill waiting for us. He followed this routine for years. Being kids, it didn't take long for us to realize that Micky would make sure the bus waited, so why hurry? Tom Kenny was our driver for years, and one couldn't ask for a better person. Along with his driving ability-ty, he was great with children. With Tom at the wheel, we arrived safely. Once a month, when Tom got paid, he would stop at the general store and buy us candy. We looked forward to that treat, and we made sure we rode the bus that day, if no other.

In September and October, the farm kids got to take a lot of days off school to do chores such as picking potatoes and cutting corn. We ground the corn into silage, as we did the hay, to get as much in the

59

silos as possible. This task took a week or so to do. Cutting corn was a backbreaking job, which we did by hand with sickles. Then we ground it up and blew it into the silo. Wally and I were the youngest, and we had to tamp down the silage, like they had, to get as much in the silo as possible. Tamping down the corn was a sticky job because of the syrup in it. When we were through, we were a mess. During potato season, we were out of school a month or more.

We had a potato digger that was drawn by horses, but the ground was very heavy at that time of year. The younger kids picked the potatoes, while Johnny and Dad hauled and stored them. We also sold some right from the field. As we got older, we were able to pick potatoes for other farmers, for money, and the job didn't seem as hard as it was when we worked at home.

Once again, we returned to school, but our weekends were full of such activities as cutting wood for the upcoming winter. In the early days, we cut down trees, hauled them home, and cut them up by hand. Later, when we got a tractor, we had a sewing machine for the front of it, which ran it off of the tractor's power. That machine was an answer to a prayer. We cut wood, cleared the land, and piled the brush to let it dry during the winter. In the spring, we burned it. In the summer, Dad pulled up the tree stumps.

In the fall, we cut Christmas trees until the first of December. We would cut the first group of trees and put them in the mud by the creek so they wouldn't dry out and lose their needles. The Christmas trees were going to city folk, and they wouldn't be used until Christmas. When we cut down the trees, we followed Dad around. When he cut one down, we dragged it into the clearing to be picked up later.

Of course, these trees were never good enough to put in our home for the holidays, but they were in good enough shape to sell. Now that I'm on the other side of the fence, I've had a taste of the selection the city folks had. To sell the trees, we had to tie the limbs with swine to keep them firm and looking good, at least until the customers bought them.

Along with the trees, we cut brushes to make blankets. We tied it by weaving the limbs together with twine to keep them together. The blankets were sent to the big cities and used to cover the graves in the cemeteries. We didn't actually make the blankets. We only tied the bundles for those who did make them. The people who made the blankets started weaving in November, so they were ready by the first of the year. Later, people found out the blankets didn't do that much good, and they no longer use them.

Between the trees and the brush, we made enough money for Christmas. Even if I didn't get everything I wanted, I got all I needed, and then some.

During October, we also took a little time out to go bird hunting. I enjoyed the sport even though I didn't hunt much. Girls didn't do things like that back then. Johnny was the hunter in our family. I never got a license, since we were hunting on our own property, and I was under sixteen years old. Bird season lasted the month of October, so while cutting trees and brushing, we always carried a .22-caliber rifle or a four-ten shotgun. We got a lot of birds during the month. Johnny got the most; he was the best shot.

We also had bird dogs through the years, but Micky outlasted them all. Though he was never a bird dog, he still wanted to go hunting. So, we took him, but after the first shot was fired, he hightailed it home. He always liked coming along the first time, and he would tree the birds. We had to be good shots, because Micky only helped us with the first bird of the day.

We had another dog, Sparky. He was a good bird dog, even if he was a mixed breed. Unlike most of the pure-bred dogs that were raised in our area, Sparky needed little training. He was always ready and rearing to go. He became mean, however, because he was very teased. He had a temper that wouldn't quit, and one day he bit the man who came to care for the cows. Pat saw him coming and took out the wooden leg he had received in the war. When Sparky bit into the wooden leg, he was so embarrassed he turned and hid.

I loved to walk through the woods in the fall of the year. The leaves were in full color, and the animals were getting ready for the long winter ahead. By the end of October, most of the leaves had fallen from the trees, and it was much easier to spot the birds. I shot my share of birds, but never as many as Johnny. As long as I could be outdoors, however, I was satisfied, and as I got older, I was able to hunt more and more.

The end of October brought the first of the holidays, Halloween. We didn't do a lot that day; it wasn't one of our big holidays. It wasn't because we didn't' do anything. It was because we lived so far from town it wasn't worth the walk. Life wasn't like it is today when we can hop into a car and go.

At school, each classroom had a party, and we marched in a parade through town to the local grocery store. When we arrived, we all got candy. All we had to do was dress up and walk in the parade. I didn't dress up much. I would put a paper sack over my head, cut out the eyes and mouth, and maybe color it a bit. The only reason I did that much was to get the candy. In those days, if I had joined in the fun and activities, it would have been a lot better for me. I have only myself to blame for missing out on those things.

November brought snow, and most of the time we had snow for Thanksgiving. Being hunters, we always looked forward to a light snow fall in November. The snow made it easier to track the deer. Deer hunting also interested me, and though I never got a license I was still able to hunt. I got a few deer, but most of the time I was the one chosen to drive them out of the swamp so someone else could shoot them. During November, the deer stayed in the thickets in or near the swamp. When it was cold or snowy, these areas offered the best protection from the elements.

In our area, the hunting season lasted only fifteen days in November, and during that time we could shoot only the bucks. There was never a doe season like some parts of the country have today. During that short season, we had a lot of hunters in our area. Most of them came from out of town or out of state. Many came from the Lower Peninsula, which was about a hundred miles away. The trip was so long because at that time, they had to cross the Great Lakes by ferry. Since there were so many of them, they also had to wait their turn to board the ferry. Sometimes they waited twenty hours in line while a gas truck refueled the cars. None dared leave and lost their place.

Through the years, many farmers posted their land because there were so many accidents. Some hunters shot at every sound, thinking or hoping it was a deer. Now and then that sound was another hunter, and the one who was killed always seemed to be a local man and one of our neighbors, which didn't sell with the hometown folks.

Sally and Micky, our faithful dogs, 1950s

Rowdy and Me, 1950s

Rev. and Mrs. Wickstrom, 1950s

Pine Mountain Ski Slide

Our high school in Felck 1950-1954

The Knott Family

Joyce and John

Judy, Marion, Gary, Kenneth, and Gordy

The hunters would tie their deer to the front fenders of their cars or trucks and haul them home to show off, I'm sure. Some of the bucks and beautiful racks, which was more important than the meat. The bigger the rack, the more their kill meant to them.

Thanksgiving came right in the middle of deer season. It was a very important holiday for us because even in the hard times, we always had a lot for which to be thankful. We always had a big dinner at our church on the Saturday following Thanksgiving. We invited the hunters from all over the area who wanted a good, home-cooked meal. Even in all my travels through the years, I found none who cooked like the Swedish ladies. Every family from the church chipped in, and so did we. And as we grew older, we helped in the kitchen. Marion always worked in the kitchen, and through the years, she never slowed her pace in helping others. I never became a cook; the best I ever did was set clear tables and help serve the meal.

One year, we thought all the chickens had been picked, cleaned, stuffed and put in the oven, but it wasn't long before we knew what we had done, or not done. One chicken had gotten by with its original insides, not the stuffing. The kitchen was in the basement of the church, and the smell seemed to go through the whole place. All the food was cooked at the church, except for the pies and cakes.

There would be at least three hundred hunters or more, and they would come and go during the evening since the supper was served for four or five hours. This dinner was an annual event at our church for years.

Not only did we have a great meal at the church, every family had a wonderful meal for Thanksgiving. We were no exception. On Thanksgiving Day, we didn't do anything except the chores that had to be done. We would cook for days to prepare for this one day.

Marion and Anna would bake pies, cakes, and bread. Then, on Thanksgiving Day they would get up early and put the chicken in the oven. In no time, we could smell the aroma all through the house, we didn't have turkey since we had a coop full of chickens.

Marion and Anna could cook with the best of them when they were only teenagers. They had a lot of practice. As I look back, I realize they, along with Johnny, grew up a lot faster than they should have. They had no choice, nor did we, the younger ones. We all grew up quickly since responsibility came to each of us at an early age, but more to the older ones.

As the dinner approached, I always looked forward to it. I am of Swedish descent, and I believe we were put on this earth for hard work and to be good cooks. There were very few skinny Swedes and not many lazy ones, I am proud to say.

Then came December, with the thrill of the Christmas holiday fast approaching. Even after all these years, Christmas is my favorite holiday. Getting together with friends and relatives and sharing whatever we have is a joy in itself. Of course, to a child, the gifts play a very important part of the holiday season.

The month of December was very busy at home, church, and school. In school, we were all included in the Christmas program, especially the younger students. We decorated the classrooms and drew names. The last day of school, we had a party in the afternoon and exchanged gifts before going home for the holidays. There wasn't much studying during the month of December. Most of the time was spent practicing for the Christmas pro-gram, which our parents and families came to watch us perform. In little towns like Foster City, everyone turned out for such events. It was a chance for parents to visit with others and brag a bit about their children.

Then life changed. In 1941, the war came. I wasn't very old, but I knew something terrible had happened that would affect us for years to come. A lot of young men and women never came home, and their passing took away a little part of us.

We have gone through two wars since. Have we learned anything? As I look back, I wonder how much we appreciate the sacrifices our servicemen and women made, or have we forgotten? Let's hope and pray we never forget that those men and women gave of themselves so we might remain free and help others to enjoy the same freedom. Do we have the guts today to stand and fight for our country like the young people who went before us? Let's hope and pray that if the need arose, we, too, would rise to the occasion. So far, each generation has risen to the call and done it with honor. So, with honor, let's recognize all those who did their part to keep us free.

With the war on and with our living so close to the Soo Locks, we had blackouts, that is, lights out at night. If we needed light, we hung heavy blankets over the windows so the light couldn't be seen from the outside. Of course, being so young I just knew we would be bombed someday, but thank God, we never were. I don't think we were in any real danger, but we never knew for sure.

Along with the war came the different rations. We had stamps for everything: sugar, coffee, shoes, tires, and gas. Since we couldn't afford to go much, we didn't notice the gas shortage as much as the others. As farmers, we were allotted a certain amount for gas. Since we didn't have a tractor at the time, we were able to use it in our car. In place of sugar, we were able to get as much powdered sugar as we wanted, which was better than no sugar at all, I guess. I loved sugar on everything possible. There was a shortage of coffee, but that didn't bother me. I was too young to drink it.

The war dragged on, and with its end came the heroes. One great hero was Oscar Johnson, my sister Marion's future brother-in-law. He was welcomed by all. We kids sat on the hillside and watched the parade come through our town. It was the event of the year. I guess it was about the best thing that ever took place in Foster City. In the parade to honor Oscar was the Honor Guard, their full colors proudly flowing in the breeze. Oscar was awarded the Congressional Medal of Honor, which had been presented to him by the President of the United States. Oscar was a hometown boy, and that's what mattered. I suppose we all envied him and his family a little whether we wanted to admit it or not. He was someone special, and we were just normal people.

There are a lot of heroes today. They may not have ever fought in a war, but that doesn't mean they are not heroes. They help others daily and do their part to make this world a better place to live. Those who died fighting died with no less dignity than those who returned as heroes. In a way, they were all heroes.

Winter arrived on the twenty-first of December, but it felt as if winter had been around for a month. We had cold weather and snow to prove it. After the first of the year, it really got cold, and it stayed that way.

CHAPTER FIVE
THE WINTER SEASON

As the seasons change, so do the people. If we could turn back the clock, how much would we change if we could? I often wonder if it would be any better the second time. Changes came and went, and I survived. As I look back, I realize I had it better than I thought at the time. It is said that "youth is wasted on the young," and there is something to be said about that.

School would close, and once again it was Christmas vacation. I always looked forward to school being closed; the reason didn't matter. I didn't like school, which was the gist of it, but I got better as the years came and went.

Every Saturday in December we had to practice for our Sunday school Christmas program. It was a time to get together, and a time of hard work and fun. I liked the singing, and, of course, we did a lot of that. I wasn't very good at it, but no one could say I didn't try.

Just about the time I began to build a bit of confidence, I got another slap in the face. One Saturday, the music teacher pulled me aside during practice. I should have known something was wrong. She asked me not to sing and to just move my lips. I didn't know what to do. I wanted to run away but knew I couldn't let Dad down. He expected us to be up there singing and doing our parts. She didn't want me to spoil the songs. I wasn't the best singer in the group, but I am also sure I wasn't the only one who couldn't carry a tune.

I returned to the stage, and it was all I could do to keep back the tears. The rest of the kids just stood there and sang away. Things that happen in our childhood are carried with us through life no matter what people say.

The next event was sending Christmas cards to everyone in town and to the relatives who lived out of town. We received many cards, too.

The winter was quite restful. The crops were in, and God put the ground to rest under a blanket of snow. My care seemed to disappear at that time of year. A person could gain ten to fifteen pounds over the holidays. People dropped in, and we went to visit.

While cutting trees in the fall, we always looked for one for us. We had to have the best and biggest in the woods. We would end up liking three or four trees, and Dad would have to go out and get a good one for use.

We made a lot of decorations, including evergreen boughs for the inside of the house, then, of course, there were the candles.

After the tree was up and decorated, we put the candle holders on the limbs. Then we installed the candles, which were about the size of birthday candles. They came in different colors, and they burned very quickly. We were forever putting new candles on the tree, and there was always someone sitting around watching the candles burn. If one of us couldn't be there, we didn't light them. They were dangerous, and if they caught the tree on fire, that would be the end of our Christmas and maybe the whole house. We had to be very careful.

A few days before Christmas, Dad would go to Iron Mountain to shop. He would have the store wrap the gifts, unless they were skis. One year we got a toboggan, which the shopkeepers were unable to wrap, and, of course, some gifts came from Santa Claus. Like all children, Santa made his stop at our house, too. We used to pick at our gifts ahead of time, and we got pretty good at re-wrapping so Dad wouldn't notice. I'm sure he never checked the gifts that closely, but we couldn't take any chances. On Christmas Eve, we would look so surprised, even if we knew ahead of time what we were to receive.

The animals needed to be tended even on holidays. While we were busy caring for the livestock, Santa Claus would make his yearly visit. Of course, we never saw him. When the chores were done and we returned to the house, the gifts were under the tree. The Christmas season wasn't like it is today when Santa comes to town weeks before Christmas Eve to see all the children. He must have a lot of helpers.

We had chores to do outside and inside. One of the worst, in my opinion, was cleaning the lamps, and they had to be extra clean for Christmas evening. Marion and Anna spent all day in the kitchen preparing the evening meal. The rest of us would set the table and clean up afterward.

We had chicken and Luft fish, a favorite entrée of the Swedish people. The tradition had been carried to America from the old country, and it continued through the generations. When you could cook the fish and make white gravy, then, and only then, you were considered a Swedish cook.

When everything was ready and the table was set, we sat down at one of the best meals of the year. We looked forward to that meal and we thanked God for all He has given us throughout the year. We knew He was our help and comfort, which was a blessing in itself. We dug into the mouthwatering meal. The only part of the meal I didn't like was the vegetables. I washed them down with milk. During those early days, I drank a lot of milk.

We finished our supper, as we called it. In those days, dinner took place at noon, and supper was served in the evening. The time after supper was our special time. Everyone and everything were in harmony. The night was so special in many ways.

After the meal, the dishes were done, the kitchen was cleaned, and it was time to open our presents, which was the highlight of the evening even if we did know what we were about to receive, having peeked time and again beforehand. We usually got skates, skis, or other winter-related items we could enjoy in the months to come. We didn't always get what we wanted, but we always got enough. Dad never had favorites, but with six children, I guess he couldn't.

When we got skis, it was great fun to go out into the crisp, cold air and to be blessed with the great northern lights, which lit up the sky almost as if it were day. The northern lights are hard to imagine unless you've seen them and enjoyed them. They are another example of God's handiwork.

With hills all around us, there was no trouble finding a place to ski. We all just had fun sharing skis. We didn't have much choice, really. It was share or not ski, as plain as that.

After a few hours of enjoying our gifts, we would get ready to go to church. The midnight service always brought in Christmas Day, and it seemed to bring a new meaning to the new year. Many people made this service a social event.

On Christmas Day, morning came early since we didn't get to bed until very late the night before, but it was only once a year. Again, we had to care for the animals. At times like that, I wished I were a city kid and could sleep in, but then again, the sooner we got our chores done, the sooner we could do whatever we wanted with the rest of the day.

We had our big meal on Christmas Eve, so the next day, we just lay around eating leftovers. It was fun. We could make any kind of snack we wanted, and I devoured the sweets.

After we finished the chores, we went skating on the river. A few shovelfuls of snow cleared the ice, and we were ready to skate. If we went in the evening, we could take a tire or two. All we had to do was strike a match, and we had enough heat and light for miles around. Every once in a while, we got brave and got too close to the edge of the ice or to the rapids, where there was no ice. There aren't enough words to describe the fear of drowning and freezing. If we fell in, the water was cold, and I mean COLD! By the time we got home, our clothes were stiff, and we weren't much better off.

Our Christmas Sunday school program was presented on Christmas evening, and we all took part, especially the young people. As the kids got older, they only sang in the choir. The teachers put in a lot of time each year making costumes and helping to decorate the church. Their biggest job was keeping the children quiet and reminding them of their parts.

The teachers had great responsibility for training them in the way they should go since a lot of families weren't interested in God or His ways. Many children came to church, but their parents only came for special occasions such as Christmas, Easter, or a funeral. A lot of people are like that today. They only go to church at special times or when they need God's help.

The parents burst with pride as their children performed, whether they had a bit part or not. The Sunday school and the teachers gave a gift to each of the children in their classes. Children also received a pin for perfect attendance. I received a pin for six years.

Then came December 26th, and everything went back to normal. I am not sure what I expected to happen, but we went back to the farm routine. We were still on vacation, though, and that was a consolation of sorts. We now had New Year's Day to which we could look forward.

Since we didn't have electricity, there wasn't much to do in the evenings. We would gather around the dining table and play whatever games we received for Christmas. Since darkness came early in the evening, we couldn't play outside unless the moon or the northern lights lit up the sky.

The week between Christmas and the New Year was slow. It was sort of a letdown for me since I had high spirits before Christmas, then, nothing.

On New Year's Eve, we once again got ready for church. Our church brought in the new year as it should be done. There aren't many churches today that still bring in the new year, but I think we still have a need for them to do so.

All during the holidays, we received many Christmas cards, and we kept them in a big, glass bowl. It was fun sorting through them to see who had sent what. There were some homemade cards, and we used to laugh and think the senders were cheap because they made their own. Maybe they were, who knows? Back then, most of our things were homemade, and Christmas was one time it was nice to get store-bought cards.

During the winter, there was nothing much to do, and it was easy to get into things. One day, Wally and I were fighting over the bowl of Christmas cards. I was running with it, and I tripped. The bowl broke and cut my leg, and I mean cut! This injury wasn't like those I'd received in years past, when I got a scratch or two. This injury was serious. Dad was close by, and he came running to see what had happened. He wasted no time picking me up and putting me on the bed to see how bad the cut was. All I could think about was the fact that I had done it again, and this time might be my last. The way I was bleeding, I was sure to die.

The only thing to do was to take me to Nurse Carlson. We didn't have enough time to take her to our house. Anna was a big help in comforting me. She quickly grabbed a rag and tied it around my leg, making a tourniquet to stop the bleeding. She stayed right there, calming me down while Johnny ran out to the barn to harness the horse and hook him to the sled that would take us down the hill.

Dad, Anna, and I jumped into the sled and flew down the hill. I was wrapped in a blanket since it was the middle of winter, and it got cold that time of year. Once in the car, Dad drove to Nurse Carlson's and in no time, we were at her front door. At the time, we did not know how serious the cut was, and I am thankful for that. Had we known, we would have been a lot more worried, if that were possible.

As she opened the door, Dad rushed in with me in his arms and laid me on the couch. Even at her young age, Anne was a great help to me from home to hospital.

Nurse Carlson took a good look at the wound and cleaned it. She could see I would have to go to the hospital. I thought at first, she would take care of it when she brought out the whiskey bottle to help me with the pain, but she wouldn't attempt it. Once again, we were on the road, but this time we were in her car, which had a heater and was more comfortable.

Christmas dinner in the 1950s

After what seemed like hours, we arrived at the Iron Mountain General Hospital, a forty-mile ride. The hospital really scared me. I thought it was the last stop before one moved to the hereafter. The hospital was where Mom went before she passed away years before. I knew we'd gone there for a different reason, but to my way of thinking, as a ten-year-old, the reason didn't matter as they wheeled me into the emergency room.

The nurses went to work getting me ready for surgery. The fancy equipment and bright lights were things I had never seen before. I was scared as I lay on the table waiting for whatever was next, but the nurses, with their friendly manners, helped me through it.

In the operating room, the nurses got ready for the doctor, but they still took some time to offer words of comfort. I am sure they could see how scared I was.

When everything was ready, they administered the ether, which was the anesthesia that was used in the early 1940s. When the doctor came in, he asked me to count from ten to one. I didn't finish counting before I was out like a light. Within a few hours, everything was sewn up neatly and trimly. The cut on my leg was eleven inches long and needed thirty-three stitches.

I had to stay in the hospital the rest of the afternoon, but since there were no extra beds, I was left in the hallway to recover. The nurses gave me a lot of attention. I was thirsty, and all I wanted was a glass of water, which was a no-no. I wanted water, and I did not know the trouble I was about to get into. A little nurse's aide came along. I don't know if she didn't know my situation or if she just felt sorry for me, but she went and got me one of the nicest looking glasses of water I had ever seen. I took one drink and got sick in no time flat.

The doctor came by, saw my condition, and knew right away what had happened. He wasted no time finding out who had given me the water. I felt sorry for the little nurse's aide because when he was through talking to her, she must have felt like two cents.

They let me go home with Dad that evening because of the lack of beds. I was put in the car, and away we went to Foster City. There was never a town that looked so good as we approached the valley with its peaceful snow and Cold, crisp wind lightly blowing. It was nice to be home again with the family that meant so much to me. Once again, God had been looking over my shoulder, and He helped me make it through another milestone in my life.

When I first arrived home, Dad carried me wherever I needed to go, the dinner table and back to bed. I stayed in bed most of the time for the first few weeks. With the busy life on the farm, my brothers and sisters did not have a lot of time for me. They had chores and all. The worst time was when school started again after the holidays. The house was so empty with only Dad and me, and he was outside much of the time doing chores or working in the woods. I was left alone in the house most of the day. He came home for lunch, and he checked on me periodically, but otherwise, I was alone. We didn't have TV, and there wasn't much on the radio.

I visited the doctor in a month or so, and I was able to go back to school. I was tired of staying home.

Kids are very inquisitive, and they wanted to see what the cut looked like. I showed them because no one had ever seen a cut like mine. I would unwrap the leg in the restroom to show it off, then rewrap it, but when I went back to the doctor, he knew right away that I had unwrapped it. I thought I could fool him. The unwrapping and rewrapping did not help the healing process, so, to this day, I have a big scar, which, had I left the wound alone, would have been a small remembrance of the accident.

I was the center of attention with the kids at school, and I wanted the experience to last as long as possible. Before long, this time would pass, and I would be in the background again. I wanted to enjoy it while it lasted.

During the winter, with all the snow, we had to plow our road, the walkway to the house, and the paths to the other building. Dad made a plow out of two planks and a cross board. He would sit on the cross board to provide the weight that was necessary to keep the plow down; otherwise, the plow would go right over the top of the snow. This contraption, too, was drawn by horses. It had snowed enough to cover the fence posts and a lot of bushes by the time the winter was over.

We also got a lot of days off from school because of the cold weather. When it got down to twenty below or more, the schools didn't open their doors. Some winters we get weeks off at a time. When the winters were mild, we were lucky to get just a few days off.

With the leaves off the trees, we could see the whole town from our living room window. It was nice because we could see the school bus for miles before it got to our stop. That way, we didn't have to stand in the cold.

Through the cold winters, our houses weren't very comfortable. Most weren't insulated, so a lot of the heat went out around the windows and doors or through the roof. There wasn't a lot we could do about it in those days, and it took a lot of wood to keep the fires going all winter. The frost on the windows would be so thick we could write our names in it. When we pressed our hands on the windows, the heat would melt the ice. We put handprints all over the windows, but by the next morning, we couldn't tell where our prints had been.

When it got really cold, we all moved downstairs for the winter. We turned our living room into the girls' bedroom, and the boys slept with Dad. At least we didn't have to run up and down stairs all day, but, on the other hand, we had to keep our things picked up all the time.

It seemed as if I could never find things when I was getting ready for school. We were supposed to put everything out the evening before, but there was always something I couldn't find such as my mittens or boots. There were many times I went to school without my mittens, and I had to keep my hands in my pockets to keep them warm.

Dad was a great fire tender. He could keep the furnace going all night by banking the fire before he went to bed, and he got up early in the morning and started it up again. Our fire never went out all winter.

On those cold nights, the water pail and wash basin in the kitchen would freeze over with a thin sheet of ice. We had cold water whether we wanted it or not.

No matter how cold it got, we always liked to go skating on the river after we lit fires for heat and light and shoveled the ice. We often played hockey, but didn't have fancy equipment. We would cut a tree limb and bend it to make a hockey stick, and we cut a piece of wood about three or four inches in diameter for a puck.

At school, the janitor would flood the playground to make one of the biggest skating rinks in town. We would bring our skates to school, and at recess, we would skate and have a lot of fun.

Kids also took their skis to school. The big hill behind the school was ideal for a ski slide. We had to share our skis at home, so we never brought them to school. Some of the kids would stay after school and play, but we were farm kids, and we had too many chores to do.

One chore that seemed to come my way every evening was getting the daily newspaper. It may not seem to be much of a chore, but I had to walk a mile or so to get it, so it was a big deal. Not having a choice, I did the nightly walk. In nice weather, it was a nice walk, but in the winter, when the snow was falling and the wind was blowing, it was a nasty chore. Going downhill was easy. I would ski down, which was a fast one-way trip. The return trip was a different story. I could ski part way home, but then I had to carry my skis up the hill. I took Micky with me on these trips, because I was never too brave. I could easily scare myself with my own imagination. I imagined that someone was standing behind the low hanging branches of the old evergreen trees. I always carried a flashlight, and with Micky at my side, no one ever jumped out and grabbed me.

We also had a dentist who came to our school every year, and we could smell his office throughout the school. I was just one of the many students who hated to go to that dentist, and my teeth weren't the best, by far. He didn't have any of the modern conveniences. He had a chair, plenty of needles, a drill, and of course a nurse. A very wealthy lady had passed away and left her money in a fund that was set up to care for the children in the county. When it came to our turn to see the dentist, the nurse would send someone to take us. If there was anything good about the experience, we got out of class for an hour or so. I don't know whether it was worse going to the dentist or waiting to go, knowing my turn was coming.

One day when we were horsing around in the kitchen, we knocked down the clock, the only one we had. It fell into a coffee pot. Dad boiled his coffee in an open pot, so it quickly filled with coffee grounds and stopped running. Although we quickly rescued the clock, cleaned out the coffee grounds, and set Big Ben back on top of the stove, it never ran again. When Dad came home from the woods and found that the clock was not working because, once again, we had been fooling around, he wasn't exactly overjoyed. That clock was the only clock in the house, and he had to buy another, which didn't please him. He couldn't take the cost of the clock out of our allowances, since we didn't get allowances in the first place, but it could be taken out of our backside, and that's just what he did!

Once again, we made the trip to the woodshed and our own switch. The only place Dad ever hit us was on our butts. I don't know if it was worse waiting for Dad to come home or getting spanking. He sent me out to get a switch, so I decided to get a weak one and hope for the best. The first time he hit me, it broke. That's when the trouble started. It made him mad. He sent me back to the woodshed to get another, and this time I got a good switch and took my punishment, like I should have in the first place.

Spring came, and once again winter was behind us. It was nice to see the grass turn green and the flowers bloom again. As the years passed, and I became a teenager, things didn't get much better for me. I had a lot of lessons to learn, and I taught them the hard way, but we all had our dreams, and as long as we kept them in mind, we had a lot going for us.

During the 1940s, the school would get trees to plant in the school forest, and the students got the job. It was nice to get away from the classroom. We would take a shovel and a sack for lunch, and away we went.

One time, when the planting had been completed and we were just hanging around, the boys started picking on us. We caught one of them and took a dead snake and tied it around his waist with the knot in the back. No one would untie it until a teacher came on the stage, and, of course, he put a stop to it. No one got into trouble at that time, and we all got a good, big laugh. During times like that, I felt a part of things.

Something else we all had to try in the middle of winter was putting our tongues on the metal frame of the windmill. Of course, our tongues stuck, and in order to get loose, we peeled a large part of the skin off. Talk about something hurting! That did, and it was a foolish idea.

We had old cars, and the heaters didn't work, but I guess we were lucky they ran. When we went someplace in the winter, we had to wrap it up in blankets to keep warm. It was a good thing we didn't go too far at one time. Even a few miles was long enough.

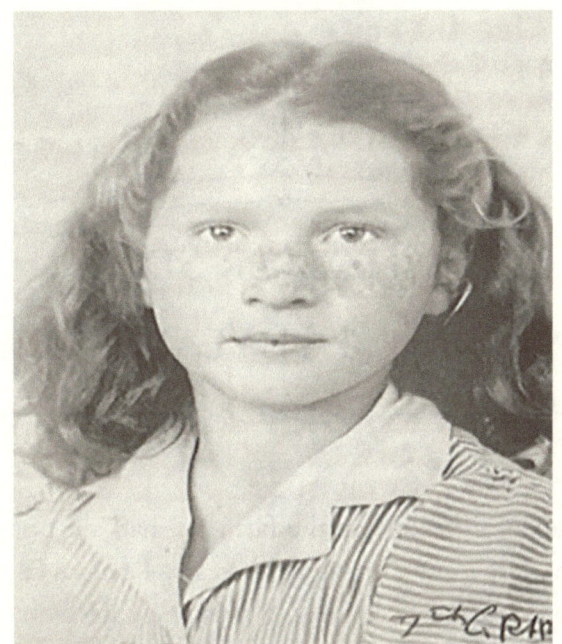

Me in 1947

Micky, our trusty dog

Chapter Six
My 4-H Years

Despite all the work on the farm, we had a little time for some extra activities. Through the years, I belonged to three 4-H clubs. The most rewarding was the café club, which was a training café for the fair in September. The other two clubs I joined were the sewing and knitting clubs, but I wasn't too interested in them. They met during the school year, while the café club met mostly in the summer.

The knitting club's meetings were held after school, so I didn't have to go home and do chores, even if it was only one night a week. There were seven or eight girls in the club, including my sister and me. The meetings included a social gathering which was better than the knitting itself. I liked gatherings like that even if I didn't have much to say or mix well.

My first obstacle was that the teacher was right-handed, and I was left-handed. Now I know that doesn't seem like much of a problem but try to teach someone to knit in the opposite direction, and see how hard it is. It was all backward to me. The teacher decided to teach me right-handed knitting, hoping to solve all our problems. The tactic may have worked, but it wasn't that easy to do. I never changed directions, even when she tried all year to help me do so.

When I was a kid, a left-handed person was even considered to be a little handicapped, but left-handed I stayed and remained today. Of course, today it doesn't matter which hand you use.

I finally mastered the knitting, at least to a certain extent. My knitting was good enough to get through the first year, and one year of that club was all I did.

I had to do two projects that year. My first project was a set of potholders, which ended up having five sides instead of four. I reworked them so many times, I wore out the yarn! My second project was a ski hat, which was more fun because it was for me, and I would be the one to benefit from it. Although it wasn't good enough to put on display, I wore it for a few years, and I was proud of it. Even though it wasn't the best. I had made it with my own hands, and that fact in itself meant a lot to me.

I also tried to make mittens, but that project was a disaster, and I never finished the mittens. As a kid. I never enjoyed knitting because I never got the hang of it. Years later, when I became an adult. I picked up the needles and was able to teach myself. I made a few projects, but nothing big.

Then came the sewing club. I did a little better with sewing, but my projects were nothing to brag about. First of all, we had to save our flour sacks. We didn't go out and buy material. Those sacks came in handy through the years. They were used for blouses and garments. The white sacks were used for dish towels and other household articles.

I didn't have much trouble cutting out the fabric for the towels or even using the pattern for an apron. I even got so I knew what I was doing, but when it came to using the sewing machine, that was a different story. We had no electricity at home, so we used a treadle machine. At school, we used electric sewing machines, which was an altogether different experience. I tore my stitches out so many times, I was lucky to have any material left before I got a project right. My project took from October through May to complete, and as with knitting club, the sewing club met once a week and included social gathering of sorts.

I don't believe anyone tried harder than I did to make a perfect project, but no one could tell by the way it turned out for me. I even prayed about my efforts. I expected God to correct my mistakes for me. I guess I thought He could just zap my project, and it would turn out perfectly. Of course, it didn't work out that way, but through the experience I learned what patience was all about, even though it didn't help much at the time. Even today, patience is one of my short suits, but I'm working on it.

Then came the day that made all my efforts worthwhile. The day was 4-H Day, which was a county-wide event that was held in Iron Mountain during the month of May, just before school let out. 4-H Day was always held on a Saturday, and it lasted all day. We always went to the event on the school bus; otherwise, a lot of us wouldn't have been able to go. There was no other transportation.

We sat through a dress show and a lot of speeches about the importance of 4-H clubs in communities. Through the years, I know the club has helped a lot of youngsters, including me. Perhaps I wouldn't have thought the speeches were so boring if I had received some recognition. It wasn't as if I deserved recognition and had been passed by. I just wasn't good enough to receive any rewards. It would have been unfair if I had received one. My sister, Marion, and her future husband, Kenneth, were very active in the 4-H clubs in Foster City. In later years, they received recognition for their efforts, and they deserved it.

After a few hours of these activities, some of us girls got bored and wanted to do something else. Since there were so many people around, no one would miss us. We made an appearance, then we slipped out of the auditorium with one the wiser. At first, we walked around town window shopping. None of us had any money. Then we were struck by the idea of going to a movie. Most of us had never been to a theater, and it was a new experience for us. I had such a guilty conscience about going, and now I am not sure why. Was it because I was supposed to be at the 4-H meeting, was it because of my religious beliefs? I was taught in Sunday school that going to a movie was a sin, and this teaching was hard for me to shake, believe me. Under that kind of pressure, I did not enjoy the movie. I was always looking over my shoulder. The best thing about it was that no one missed us. That's how important we were, and since I didn't receive any rewards, I didn't worry about it.

There were also other club's girls could join, which included the canning and gardening clubs. Neither of these activities interested me in the least. I did not enjoy canning, housework, or gardening when I had to do those jobs at home. The only other club was the café club, and I stayed with that club for six or more years.

I was excited about joining the café club, and I couldn't wait until I was old enough. I knew I could do a lot better in that club than I had in previous clubs. Even though it entailed a lot of hard work, I didn't mind. When people like what they are doing, they don't mind how much work a project involves.

Kenneth was our 4-H leader for the years I was in the café club. He was very understanding, and he cared about the members. He helped us with any and all of our problems, and he was a friend to each of us. I guess having Kenneth for a leader helped me, too, since he was fond of my sister, Marion. A few years later, they were married. Kenneth's family had one of the biggest farms in the area, and they were active in our church.

I joined the club at the ripe old age of ten. The members' ages ranged from ten years to sixteen years old.

In my first year as a member, I started with a calf. Since we lived on a dairy farm, there were a lot of calves from which to choose; however, it was difficult to make the right choice. I liked some of the calves for their markings, not their shapes, and shape is the most important feature in showing cattle at a fair. Dad helped us to pick out the animal best suited to show. Then we were ready for the training sessions, which would last all summer. We worked with our calves in the evenings only, since we still had our other chores to do. All the training paid off in September, over the Labor Day weekend.

It was a long road to the county fair, but it was worth it. At least, I thought so at that time. First of all, we had to make our halters out of rope, which we did at club meetings during the early spring.

We had to get our calves used to a halter, and that was a job in itself. The animals had never even had a rope around their necks before, let alone a halter. They were only two or three months old when we began working with them. When they were used to the halter, we began to train them.

Ann and Wally with some of the calves available for selection

The training took a lot of time and practice because the calves weren't interested in performing while their counterparts were busy grazing in the cool of the evening. They would either pull us all over the farm, or they wouldn't move at all. I don't know which experience was worse. A stubborn mule had nothing over those calves, but extra treats, such as feed or apples, did the trick most of the time. When we ran out of feed in the late summer, we had to catch the calves the same way we did the horses. They were just as gullible at first, but it didn't take them long to figure out we had sand in the bucket. We walked them around the barnyard for hours, until they learned to follow us and to stand where we wanted them to stand. Some of the calves were so wild, all we could do for the first month or so was hang on until they became tired or ran through the bushes or up and down the hills. There were times we were so scratched up we looked as if we had been in a fight. We never let go of the halter rope, if that were possible, but sometimes we didn't have a choice. I was determined to win the rounds, and I did. We trained our calves three or four evenings a week, and we had a long summer to which we could look forward.

In August, Kenneth came around to all the members' farms and clipped the calves. The calves would be clipped between their horns and around their ears and tails. The end of the tail was left long so we could curl it at fair time. The clippers were hand powered, and one of us had to turn the handle as fast as possible to create enough power to run the clippers. I got the job while the guys did the clipping. Clipping the calves was the first step in preparing for the fair. We cut the calves' hair early in order to give it time to grow out and look good. We trained the calves until fair time because they never got too much training.

The county fair was always held over Labor Day weekend. It started on Friday. The county would send trucks to pick up the 4-H members' cattle for the fair, which was a free service to all 4-H members.

We led our calves to the center of Foster City in the morning and waited for the trucks to arrive. Then the fun started! Animals that had never left the farm before were about to be loaded into big county trucks, which backed up against a bank since we didn't have a ramp. Some of the calves didn't want to get into the trucks by themselves, but with the few men around, it didn't make much difference. The men would just carry them on.

The 4-H boys, including my brothers, would ride on the trucks with the cattle in order to help unload them when they got to the fair and to watch them enroute. The boys also got to stay at the fair and take care of the cattle. In those days, girls did not participate in this part of the fair. So, guess who got the job of doing the chores back at the farm. We girls!

A style show took place at the fair on Sunday afternoon. I was not interested in it. I did not attend, and I was never in it. The better projects from the different sewing clubs were put on display. None of them were mine. I remember how well Marion, Anna, and Ruthie could sew, and they continued to sew through the years. I didn't take sewing seriously even when I had children for whom to sew, but then, my sisters mastered a lot of skills like that. Since I wasn't interested, I didn't really try that hard.

It was a nice change, doing the boys' chores those few days Johnny and Wally were at the fair. During that time, Dad and we girls did everything inside and outside the house. It was a busy time in the Swanson household, as it was for all 4-H families. We fed the cows, milked them, and bedded them down for the night. Then we sat down for a late supper and fell into bed. Even then, it was hard to fall asleep. We were being excited about the next day. We were wide awake until 5:00 A.M., and once again we did the chores as quickly as we could so we could be on our way. The county fair was the big event for the year.

Early Saturday morning, when we went to get the cows for the milking, there was always frost or heavy dew on the ground from the chill in the air. I loved to walk through the pasture and make trails in the dew or frost. It was so peaceful in the morning. It was nice being by myself. Since I was from a large family, times alone were few, so when there was a chance to be alone, I took advantage of it.

When we finished with the cows and the milking, we had to care for the rest of the farm animals, the horses, the pigs, and those crazy chickens. When we were in a hurry to go somewhere, it always seemed as if things went wrong at the last minute. Just about the time we were ready to drive out of the yard, one of the horses or cows would get out or something else would happen, but we always made it to the fair on time.

Once we piled into the car with our lunch baskets and drinks, we were on our way. I looked forward to the fair. It was the main event of the year. Once we got there, along with the rest of the club members, we had to clean our animals and get them ready for judging.

Open class was in the morning, which meant that all the farmers' and 4-H members' animals were judged together. Usually, we didn't fare too well. There were farmers who had the same cattle year after year, and they brought their whole herd. Most 4-Hers had one or two animals. In the afternoon, however, the competition was strictly for the 4-H clubs in the county, but the local farmers showed off their herds, which was good advertising for their future sale. The same farmers always walked off with top ribbons, but I got my share of ribbons through the years. Things like prize ribbons meant a lot to me.

While waiting to go into the judging ring, I used to walk my calf to keep her from lying down and getting dirty again and to keep us both occupied. This competition was one of the times I was proud to take my place with the rest of the kids in the ring. I knew I was as good as anyone else there. I don't know why I couldn't take this feeling of confidence into other aspects of my life at that time.

Then came my time to enter the ring. I was proud of all my hard work, and I knew I could make the animal do what I wanted, but sometimes it didn't turn out the way I planned it. Some of the judges were nice and friendly. Others carried a stick and poked at the animals to make them jump. Sometimes I thought they poked at them just to see how well we handled the animals. They let their position as judges go to their heads. I was always pretty lucky and handled my animal pretty well. At least, it didn't get away from me like some other contestants' animals did.

One year I gave the judge the wrong age of my calf, and he made me go into another class. I was sent to the next class, where the animals were older, and I didn't have a chance. I ended up in the last place. I was so embarrassed. I knew it was my fault, but even with that mistake, I never thought of quitting.

During the lunch break, we all ate together and shared what we had. Mrs. Johnson, Kenneth's mother, made the best fried chicken and potato salad. There was always plenty of food for everyone since Marion and Anna had also made a lot. We always had Kool-Aid to drink, and now and then, we brought pop, which was a real treat. I know it sounds funny in this day and age to say a bottle of pop was a real treat.

In the afternoon there was the 4-H judging contest, where we all fared better. After the judging was over, we had a few hours or so before we went home. Dad would give us a few dollars, and down the midway we would go. It didn't take me long to spend it. I always wanted to win one of those big Teddy Bears, but I never did, and I never gave up trying.

I remember one time I tried to win a bear by throwing rings over the top of Coke bottles. The rings didn't go because they didn't fit, but being kids, we didn't know that. Finally, a farmer from Foster City, who had been watching, came to our rescue. He challenged the booth's operator to put the rings over the bottles, which he couldn't do. He got mad and gave us each a nice stuffed animal, which was the only one we ever won. We were told never to go back to that booth, and, of course, we never did. The farmer explained to us that the booths were a rip-off. To this day, I seldom try any of those games. I'll go to the store for what I want, where it is cheaper.

While I spent most of my money on games and food, I kept enough for one ride on the merry-go-round. I always enjoyed that ride, even when I got older. In no time, I was broke, and it wasn't any use asking Dad for more money. Once in a while, however, he gave us more. It wasn't that he didn't want to; but he didn't have it to give. Caring for six children was difficult.

Once back home that evening, we went through the same routine of doing the chores. The milking took the longest by the time we were through, it was time to go to bed. I used to think about what it would be like if there were no chores. We never had a vacation or any time off.

We had a lot to do that night to get ready for bed. The next day was Sunday, and there was a parade. We had to wash and press our white pants and shirts. They were made from cotton, and they were hard to keep clean. I often thought the 4-H organization should change its colors.

Sunday afternoon, all the members from the different 4-H clubs had to parade in front of the grandstand. The bands would march with us, and with the noise, it was hard to handle the animals. Now and then, one of them got away. Then we listened to the speakers telling us we were tomorrow's adults. Now that I am older, I realize what they were trying to tell us was important.

On Monday, there was another parade in the afternoon, and we got into the fair for free and into the grandstand to watch the horse pulling contest. I liked that event. Some of the horses were so tame, one might say they were lazy, but they were well tended. On the other hand, some of the teams had been so mistreated while they were being trained, it took three extra men to handle them. Sometimes as they were being hooked up to slide with the weight, they would literally jump into action, and sometimes they were injured if a chain came loose or if they broke their harnesses because they wouldn't stop pulling. They were so frightened. Sitting there, watching that event, we knew which horses were mistreated and which ones weren't.

Dad always let us stay at the fair for as long as possible. We enjoyed the evening when the lights came on, which created a different atmosphere. We went home an hour or so after the lights came on.

When the fair closed, all that remained were the 4-H members and their cattle. The boys had to stay and care for the animals and help with the trip back to Foster City. They were lucky to be able to stay at the fairgrounds for four days; it was like a vacation.

I am thankful that 4-H girls can do more now than they could.

The 4-H members also got to miss the first day of school. Of course, there was never much going on anyway, so it really didn't matter.

When the boys returned to Foster City, all Johnny and Wally had to do was let the animals go. They knew the way home, and I'm sure they were glad to be back.

The coming of fall brought new faces in nature, and there was always something to look forward to, especially the coming of Halloween, followed by the other holidays. Christmas was my favorite.

With my schoolbooks under my arm, I was off to school once again, and I was starting to understand that what I accomplished in life was up to me. I couldn't go around blaming others for the way I turned out. I know that a person's upbringing has something to do with it, but as a person grows older, he or she can change the results of those factors, too. I think my Dad did a good job rearing us; our Christian outlook is still the most important factor in our lives.

Chapter Seven
My Teen Years

To my surprise, as I entered my teens, there were no major changes. I am not sure what I expected. It will be my last year attending the school in Foster City. My next step would be to venture to Felch and attend high school.

At last, I started to have a few friends. One special friend was Ruthie. She always had time for me, and as time went on, we kept in touch. Ruthie and her family had moved to Foster City from Chicago.

The first in our family to leave home was Marion, and, oh, how I missed her. She got married in June and moved across town, so we still saw her often. Marion married Kenneth Johnson, whose family had been long-time residents in the area.

After a year or so, Marion and Kenneth had a daughter, Judy. She arrived on the scene early, but she was a healthy child. Later, Marion and Kenneth had two boys, Gordy and Gary. They would have had four children, but the last baby boy lived only four days. He was a great loss, but God was there to help them through. God was an integral part of their family.

Marion and Kenneth were also farmers, and when the trees were bare in the winter, we could see their farm across the valley.

Another summer passed, and it was time for school again. Wally and I also attended confirmation classes, as had our sisters and brothers before us. We went to class once a week, on Saturdays during the school year. I loved to read and study the Bible. There I found out about great men and how they had sinned, as we all have, and how God was right there to help them through their hard times and to change their lives in the process. I seemed to be at home in church, and I felt good inside. I was content, and I felt important while attending a Bible study or church service. God seemed to be showing me that the things of the past were not my fault. The devil created all the sinful things on the earth, and we couldn't blame God for them. I know we can't keep sinning and asking God for help without working with him to correct our problems. We also have to do our part.

Rev. Wickstrom was the minister of our church. He had once been a log-ger, and he fit right into our way of life in Foster City. He was a big man, but he was caring and understanding. We had other ministers who came and went, but there were none like Rev. Wickstrom and his wife. His children were grown up before he came to Foster City, so we really never knew them. Mrs. Wickstrom had a beautiful voice and sang a lot in church. It seemed as if all our minister's wives sang.

Then came the holiday season, and once again we cut a Christmas tree and brush. No matter the age, I always enjoyed the coming of the holidays and all the preparation that went into them. They were a lot more than gifts and food. I began to understand the meaning of Christmas; many people never do. I had known for years that Christmas was Christ's birthday. We had learned about it in Sunday School. We learned a lot of the Old Testament stories that led up to the birth of Christ, who was the greatest gift of all.

After the Christmas holidays, we were once again in school. Things were about the same for a while. We had a teacher who should have been a college professor. We learned more in one year than most classes did in three. There was no way for us to keep up with him, but we tried to learn it all. He stayed for only one year, then he took a job in higher education. He was too educated to teach in grade school, but we all made it through even if it was hard on us.

One day while we were playing outside at school, I accidentally broke a window with a marble. It was the first time I had done anything like that, so I did not know what to do or say. Three of us girls made a pact not to say anything, and that's exactly what we did. I knew it wasn't right, but my dad was on the school board, and if he knew, he would be furious. I also learned another lesson. I had two friends who were willing to keep their mouths shut so I wouldn't get in trouble. I began to realize that a person can have true friends.

Rocks were a big part of the spring planting. Many farmers made fences out of them. As the frost left, the rocks were forced out of the ground. The only way to get rid of them was to pick them up, another job done by hand. Then we used a team of horses and a wagon to haul them away. Moving the rocks was a back-breaking job, and it was the dirtiest. We ate sand all day.

After attending confirmation classes during the school year, it was time to graduate. The next step was to become a church member. Upon graduation, we gave a presentation to the rest of the congregation, which was the first time I had to get up before a group of people. The church was full. We all had something to recite from the Bible, and I had the first Psalm. Things were looking up for me. I was getting more confident, but I still had a long way to go. Once again, my efforts were dampened when I forgot part of the Psalm, but Rev. Wickstrom was quick to help out. The main thing was that we had worked all year for this day.

When the day arrived to take pictures, we had to go to Iron Mountain. We spent the day in town and had lunch. We did our best for Rev. Wickstrom. He always tried to bring out the best in us, and his efforts worked.

Our eighth-grade graduation followed the completion of confirmation classes. At the end of May, I finished my years at Longfellow

School. I was about to move to the high school, which took in students from three townships. I looked forward to high school. It seemed as if I were always looking forward to the next step in life. I always thought my life would improve, and in some cases it did. At other times I wasn't so lucky, but we all have to keep marching in life.

Graduation was a big event in our lives, and we had looked forward to the day for a long time. In addition, graduation was an occasion when the whole town turned out to honor the students' accomplishments, great or small. It didn't matter to the town folks; they were there to honor us. The speaker was the superintendent from the high school we would attend the following year. He told us about the importance of having an education, a concept we would understand better as adults.

Our class colors were red and white. Our class flower was the apple blossom. We picked blossoms for days since every farmer in our area had an orchard. We spread them on the aisles we used to walk to the stage. There were only nine students graduating, so we all sat on stage with the guest speaker and the principal.

We had practiced our parts for days. During practice breaks, we sat around and talked. One day the music was on, and some of the students started to dance. I was also asked to dance, but there was no way I was going to. I was too self-conscious, and I thought dancing was a sin! Dancing itself wasn't wrong; it was what happened on the way to and from such events. If a person didn't have self-respect, it didn't matter where he or she was. To this day, however, I never really learned to dance.

During the summer, we would go to Norway Lake with our church group. I always stayed close enough to shore to touch bottom. I felt safer there, but as I grew older and braver, I became brave enough to swim out to the barrels, which were in water that was at least twelve to fifteen feet deep.

To a lot of people that depth of water is not deep, but it was to me. The barrels were stacked three high, so they were about four feet under water. When I swam out there, I put my foot on the barrel to rest. They were rusty and my foot went through the top of one. I couldn't get it loose, and I was stuck under the water. I knew I was dying, but, once again, God was looking over my shoulder. Kenneth was right there. He got my foot loose, and he helped me to swim to the shore. I sat on the beach and stayed there the whole summer. I never felt comfortable swimming in that lake again or in any other lake for that matter. Through the years, I have enjoyed swimming in a pool because I can see and feel the bottom.

One summer I was picked by the church to go to church camp. Our church picked two students to attend the camp, and the church paid for it! We prayed hard for my time at camp to go right. I knew God would be there, too. Attending camp was the first time I had been away from home, except for staying with my grandparents. The day came, and Rev. Wickstrom drove us to the big camp. Girls from all over the peninsula were there. I didn't realize there would be so many girls. I don't know what I expected. The camp lasted a week. We had Bible classes in the morning and activities in the afternoon such as swimming or playing ball.

When the time came to go swimming, I proudly put on the bathing suit Marion had made for me. I ran down to the lake to swim with the rest of the girls, who started to laugh when they took one look at me. They called me, "The poor little redhead."

I loved Marion, and when she had made me the suit, I was proud of it. We didn't have enough money to buy one. I was crushed. I knew how much time she had put into making the suit, but the other girls didn't know. I ran back to my room and cried deeply. I wanted to go home, but I couldn't. I had enjoyed camping up to that point, and I couldn't believe that kind of behavior could happen in a church camp.

Of course, I didn't go swimming the rest of the week. The counselor made the girls apologize, but it didn't help. I knew they really didn't mean it. After that incident, I felt as if the girls were laughing at me for everything I did. I could hardly wait for Saturday to arrive so I could go home. I never went to church camp again, or to any other camp for that matter.

If I could just make it through the next four years of high school, I thought I would be free, and my problems would be over. I thought my first year in high school would be different. I thought I was a big shot because I was in high school, but it didn't take long for that idea to fade. I found out 1 had to work at solving my problems because they didn't go away by them-selves. They would get bigger if I didn't do something about them, which was a fact of life I found out the hard way. Once again, I was at the bottom of the ladder looking up.

When fall rolled around again, we were off to school, and I was ready to get started climbing the ladder. High school wasn't too exciting for the first couple of years. I earned a C average all through school, and I am sure I could have done better, but I didn't. It's too late now to change my high school performance.

For the next four years, our class advisor was also our typing teacher. He spoke to me about the importance of typing and English. If I had known then what I know now, I would have tried a lot harder, but I can't turn back the clock.

All we can do is go on and try to improve ourselves. It is, however, a good thing we can't turn back the clock. Some of us would never move forward.

We took off the first few months of school each year to pick potatoes. After our harvest, we went to help other farmers with their crops, and now we were paid for our work, which was a bit different. The money we earned was spent to buy clothes and to purchase school pictures. In our senior year, we needed a class ring, a must for everyone. We earned ten cents a bushel, which was a good wage in the 1950s. Ruthie and I worked together. We picked two hundred bushels of potatoes a day, and our days were long, daylight to dark.

We sold the big potatoes. We used the others ourselves, boiling the dwarfs for the pigs. The cows also loved the potatoes. They roamed the fields after we picked what we could. They ate what was left behind. We also grew early potatoes, which we harvested in August and sold right from the field, so we didn't have to store them.

During my high school years, I belonged to the youth group at the church. We get

together about twice a month on Saturday evenings. We sang, played games, and had refreshments. We also had a special activity planned for each season. In winter, we went Christmas caroling. In the summer we had a candlelight service at the lake.

Again, we rode the bus to Felch to attend school. It seemed as if we were always on the bus. We rode to the grade school, then the older students would board another bus and ride to the high school.

We didn't have too many school activities at that time. Girls never played sports. I really wanted to play, but there were no teams for girls. The boys were also limited. They had baseball and basketball teams, but our school was too small to have a football team or track team.

Every morning, we gathered in the main assembly hall, which was also used for study hall and any other activity that might come up during the day. Many times, we never made it to our first, second, or third class. Our super-intendent was long winded. He could talk for hours. He should have been a politician. He spoke about the events of the day, and if there were any problems we heard about them.

On the other hand, he kept our school open for years because he was able to keep the state inspectors happy when they came to check the school. It should have been closed years before it was. Felch High School had about eighty students. Our superintendent would also do anything he could for a student. He stuck up for us no matter what he had to do. He wanted the best for us, and we got the best. We had great school spirits.

I remember my English and home economics teachers. The English teacher was also the basketball coach. When we wanted to lie back and do not have much to do, we would get him started on the events of the last game or the upcoming competition. When he wasn't talking about basketball, we learned a lot. He could do two jobs, and he did them well.

Our home economics teacher was a good cook, but she made the fanciest dishes. We were all from homes where we ate simple meals. We didn't need fancy dishes. Most of us had learned to cook at home. She was also seamstress, and she taught us well. I wasn't interested in that class, but I had no choice about attending.

Since our mother was gone, one of us was permitted to take a day off school once a week to do the washing and ironing. Ruthie didn't want to stay home very often. She enjoyed school and wanted to go to college, so she needed the best grades.

Typing was another hard class for me, but as the years passed, it was a great help. Although typing was a rough course for me, I stayed with it, and I got pretty good at it. When I received a B, I was proud. Through the years, typing became important to me in different jobs. Our typing teacher didn't grade on a curve. Students received the grade they exactly earned. My teacher used to talk to me about life. He knew I would succeed even if I didn't think I would at the time.

Success depends upon how one defines it. I wasn't sure how I defined success or what I would do with my life. Years later, I still wasn't sure.

The FFA teacher was a very nice guy, and he was good looking. Of course, back then, girls weren't allowed to be in the FFA; however, three of us tried. Life wasn't like it is today when girls can do whatever they want to do. No matter what career a girl might choose, nowadays she can just go for it and not be afraid. Girls don't have to prove anything to anyone anymore.

When we come to the end of life, will we be satisfied with what we have accomplished, or will we wish we would have done things differently? As we look back, there are things we all would like to change. That's natural, but we shouldn't keep looking back.

We all need people to talk to, and I was lucky I had a person like Marion with whom to speak and to pray.

In the early 1950s, lightning struck the old Roman Catholic church, and it burned to the ground before anyone could help. We didn't have a fire department. The sisters in the church were able to carry out most of the important items. The church used our school for services until a new church was built.

Our church, like the old Roman Catholic Church had been built years before, and it had an old-fashioned look. With the new church, there seemed to be something missing. We continued to compete with each other, however. When the Roman Catholic Church redid its front yard, our church redid its. When we put up a sign, so did the other church. This competition went on for years. It was sort of funny watching the two churches try to outdo each other. Both churches were kept in good condition and were notified by anyone who passed through Foster City.

With the closing of my second year in high school, I had a lot which to look forward to. The junior class would put on plays and take trips.

During the summer, our youth group had several activities. We held our annual candlelight service, and during an evening, in July we went to Norway Lake. We sang and prayed, then, one by one, we went down to the lake's edge and gently set a candle on the water. We secured the candles on pieces of wood so they would float. One candle made little light, but many candles made a beautiful sight, and the scene caused me to think about what I could do in life. When we all had our lights burning for the same cause, it could make a difference.

That year, we bought a tractor with rubber wheels. Many tractors back then had iron wheels, and they were hard on the blacktop roads. Now we could work from morning until night, and we didn't have to rest it like we did the horses. That summer, we got the tractor stuck many times, and the horses had to come to the rescue. They were still used for some of the chores around the farm. Dad became a mechanic in a hurry because we didn't have the money to hire someone to keep the tractor running.

One event I still don't understand. Ruthie and I were using the tractor in the field, and when we finished, we parked it in the barn. In the morning, when Dad started it up, one of the front wheels fell off. The axle was broken! I don't think Dad ever believed us, but it was okay when we parked it the night before.

There was no way we could work any place other than the farm. We all had plenty of work right there. So, with some thought, we decided to plant a crop for extra money. When we approached Dad with the idea, he was all for it. He gave us a piece of land to work to plant and harvest whatever we decided to grow.

The first two years, we planted beans. The cannery in Iron Mountain gave us the seeds. Then, cannery workers came around once a week to pick up the beans we harvested. We were excited. We were going to make some big bucks. The first year, we did pretty well. A little money was better than none. So, we grew beans for a second year, but the project got old after a while. We picked well, until we had the seed paid for, then we slacked off. By the end of the second season, Wally and I picked most of the beans because the rest of the family had other things to do. Instead of shaking the bags down to get the most in each one, we just dumped the beans in the bag so they would fill up faster. We had to pick three or four bags of beans a day. Dad helped us once in a while, which kept us going whether we wanted to or not. At our house, when one started a project, it was completed, good idea or not. It made no difference.

One year, Wally and I decided to grow cucumbers. One would think we had learned our lesson, but I guess we hadn't. The almighty dollar makes people do funny things. The cannery gave us the seed, and all we had to do was pick the cucumbers. Cannery workers would haul the cucumbers away daily.

We got until the plants started coming up and, lo and behold, so did the weeds. I had never seen so many weeds in one field. The cucumbers were worse than the beans when it came to picking them. The vegetables had to be a certain size for pickles. I don't think we sold enough cucumbers to pay for the seed. If anything, good came out of the experience, it was the fact that we had plenty of cucumbers for our dinner table. I would sit and eat them by the dozen. To this day, I eat cucumbers like candy.

Each fall, we had to get our meat ready for the winter. We butchered pigs and chickens. We had to heat the water in big barrels on an outside fire, which was handy. After killing the pigs, we quickly dipped them into the boiling water to scrape off the hair before cutting the skin. We did the chicken at the same time. They were put in the boiling water also. The feathers came off much more easily. Neither job was very pleasing to us, but after the bacon was smoked and Grandma made the head cheese, it was all worthwhile.

I guess it was around this time that I really started to grow up and see things differently. I wasn't excited about farming anymore. I enjoyed it to a certain extent, but knew I couldn't stay on the farm forever.

CHAPTER EIGHT
MY LAST YEARS

My last few years at home, farming became easier. The threshing machine and the grain binders had become outdated. What had taken a whole threshing crew to do in a week was now done by one to two men. Johnny was gone, and I helped in the fields with the haying and harvesting of grain. The haying season was easier because hay bailers and other fancy equipment came along with the tractors. The horses were put out to pasture for a rest that had been a long time coming.

A summer of chores and harvesting was over. September rolled around again, and it was time to begin the last two years of high school with all its activities, but once again, it was time for the potato harvest. We all pitched in. First, we picked our own potatoes, then we worked for the other farmers in the area. Money was important and necessary. I wanted a class ring, and in the spring, pictures would be taken for graduation. We needed photographs for relatives, friends, and, most important, our classmates. I needed a new dress for the junior/senior banquet and the upcoming class play.

We, along with other farmers, sold our potatoes to the government under the support price program, which, to me, was a big mistake because the government paid the farmers for not selling or growing crops. Some people were farmers in name only. They worked in the city and never grew a crop. It made it hard on farmers like us, real farmers who lived on the farm and worked it. Others just let the land go, and in later years, the government paid them to grow trees. As a result, the fields could no longer be used for farming.

The government bought our potatoes, put lye on them, and never sold them to keep the prices up. Before they began to put lye on them, the potatoes drew rats and other pests. Then, once the potatoes were gone, the rats moved to surrounding farms. Wally and I had to put out poison to get rid of them. Not only did we get rid of the rats, we got rid of Sparky our good, old bird dog. He got into the poison. We had tried to keep him away from it, but he was always into things, and this time was no different.

October was hunting season, and Wally and I did a lot of hunting. I've killed my share of birds and deer, but, sorry to say, I don't have a real hunting story to tell. I missed Sparky when we went hunting. He was a good bird dog. While hunting, we carried buckshot and birdshot for our shotguns. If we saw a bird, we used birdshot. A deer called for buckshot, and we got a little fresh meat.

One time Wally and I went hunting. After shooting a deer and cleaning it. Wally moved to put his knife away in its holder on the side of his boot. Not looking at what he was doing, he missed the holder and put the blade on the side of his leg. What a mess! His blood was all over but the wound looked worse than it really was. The sight of Wally's blood didn't do either of us any good, but we were close to home. I helped him to the house and tried to get the bleeding stopped. I even tried flour, but Wally ended up going to the doctor for a few stitches. Between Wally and I, there was always something happening. It kept Dad on his toes, which I'm sure he really didn't need.

By this time, only Wally and I remained at home. Ruthie had graduated and moved away to pursue a nursing career. I was left to do the housework, which included washing. I didn't like the work that much, but I had no choice.

The wash was an all-day job. Just getting the washing machine started was a chore. It was like a motorcycle with a foot peddle and all. It had an old gasoline motor. Once the water was heated on the stove and the soap put in, we would wash the clothes and rinse them by hand. The wringer caught on everything, even our hands if we weren't careful. Many people, in those days, ruined their hands and even an arm or two. The wringer had a safety lever, but it rarely worked. We dried the clothes outside in good weather. In the winter, we hung them by the furnace to dry. It seemed it took forever to dry clothes. When we weren't using the furnace to dry clothes, we were drying our mittens, etc.

December meant a month of excitement. We planned events and got things ready for the holidays. The first event was to decorate the church and go Christmas caroling, which I always enjoyed.

When it came to decorating the church, we went out to get a tree from someone's farm. The tree was at least fifteen feet high and filled the corner of the church. It reached the high ceiling. The tree took a lot of decorations, but when we were finished, it was always so pretty. We would stand around and sing and have refreshments.

Next came the caroling, with the falling of snow and the cold, crisp air nipping our faces. It was a wonderful feeling. We all wanted to sing our hearts out, and that is what we did. I was beginning to sing and feel more comfortable about it. When we finished, we went to someone's house and had refreshments. During the course of the evening someone always invited us for hot chocolate and cookies. By the end of the evening, we had more than our share of goodies.

Every home was nicely decorated and gave us a warm and cozy feeling, perfect atmosphere for the season. Before we closed the evening, we always said a prayer of thanks to God for the wonderful time and what it meant to us.

Some winters, when we ran out of firewood, we would have to cut it when the snow was waist deep. We were cold and wet by evening. The saw machine was mounted on the tractor during the fall and winter months. It was always hard to start, so we used the horse to pull it. It was one of Rowdy's jobs. He was a red animal, like out of a story book, and he was everybody's friend.

Shortcuts caused accidents. Once, I went to get Rowdy to pull the tractor to start it. The saw ran by a belt off the flywheel, which we always left on. Before I could get the horse out of the way, the tractor slid onto him and cut him to the extent. He couldn't be saved. I felt so sorry for him. I sat out in the barn with him until the man from the mink farm came to get him. He would buy any and all animals for meat. The accident didn't happen on purpose, but it had happened just the same. It didn't matter whose fault it was.

I was asked to be a Sunday school teacher, and I was thrilled that anyone would consider me for the position. Of course, I accepted, but I was scared to death at first. I was afraid I couldn't do a good job. I prayed and studied a lot, knowing I had to do both. I loved every Sunday I taught, and I learned a great deal about God and myself.

Children can do a lot for people if we let them. I had three- and four-year-olds in my class. We used the church kitchen for our classroom. I loved to tell them stories of God's love. It was a lot more fun if I told stories instead of reading them out of a book. The children took part in the class, which made it more interesting.

Another big event in our area was the ski tournament at Pine Mountain, which was held every February or early March. Pine Mountain had the biggest man-made ski jump in the world, so skiers came from everywhere to take part in the event. The Norwegians took most of the honors, but once in a while a local boy would stand out. No women took part.

Like most teenagers, I liked to go to the tournament for a two-fold reason. I loved to watch the skiers fly through the air, and I dreamed of being one of them, which never happened of course. There was also the social aspect of the event. We dressed as much like skiers as possible, much like today when attending a rodeo, and everyone wears cowboy boots, cowboy hats, and other cowboy attire. We weren't any different in those days. I was lucky to have the ski hat I had made in knitting class. Some of the kids would be all decked out. They looked more like skiers than the skiers. It was a lot of fun spending the day there. We would get a bus from Foster City and go to Pine Mountain for the day. The tournament lasted two days, but we only got to go on the first day, which was Saturday. We had to pay for the bus and driver when we took a trip like this.

Rowdy and Me

The Ski Jump at Pine Mountain

Once we got there, there was so much to see. First, there were pastry stands, which also sold hot coffee and steaming chocolate. The stands were my favorite tournament attractions. A lot of it had to do with the atmosphere I always liked to eat when I went to events such as that.

As we approached the 400-foot hill and looked up, we saw the wooden slide on top. Skiers could travel up to ninety miles per hour when they jumped, and they looked so graceful flying through the air.

I'd also like to talk about the air raids we had at school during the 1940s and 1950s. They were like the fire drills schools have today, but they were for another reason. The schools and the country had a system. If we heard one blast of the horn, everybody got under their desks since there wouldn't be time to go outside. If we heard two blasts, we had time to run out of the school building and jump into a ditch, which was about one-hundred-fifty feet from the school. It was there in case the enemy attacked. When the drills ended, I thanked God for saving America.

I often wonder why we try so hard to achieve world peace. When families can't get along, how can we expect nations to get along? We have to start at home and not at the United Nations. If we correct our family problems, the rest will fall in line.

In the spring, we planned our class play. It was a job since we had only seventeen students in our class. We all had a task to perform. Some had two or three. I didn't have the courage to try out for a part or to even think about it. I enjoyed working behind the scenes, where, I found out, we all had an important job of making the play a success. As in life, no matter how large or small the task is, we had to do our best, whether working by ourselves or in a group. Mistakes would be made, but friends and parents would overlook them and still be there for us.

The night of the play, we all dressed in our finest clothes. We went to the school early to make sure everything was ready, and we were a bit nervous, I might add. We performed in a three-act comedy, Brides to

Burn. It was a great success, and we enjoyed doing it. We raised money for our junior/senior banquet, which was held at a nice restaurant with a banquet room and all the fixings. The junior class had to pay for it, and, of course, next year, we would be the guests.

During the spring, we had a lot of cleaning up to do around the farm. When the snow was gone, we burnt brushes. We set the piles of brush on fire in the evenings, and we sat around to make sure the flames didn't get away and that all the brush burned. In a month or so, we will begin working on the farm.

We also had to clean up around the farm buildings. We burnt the old grass around the place. One day I was burning grass, and I let the fire get too close to the woods. Before I could get the fire out, it burned half the hillside. The hillside looked awful for years. Most of the trees died and had to be cut down, but the undergrowth came back the next year. I never did that again.

One day, Wally and I were told to tear down the old woodshed since it was about to collapse. We always saved the nails and lumber, but in this case, the lumber wasn't worth keeping. I took the tractor, and we tied a chain around the shed's middle post. One pulled and the building was down. We lit a match to it, and after the ashes cooled, we picked up the nails and put them in a can. When Dad saw what we did, he was disappointed in us once again. The nails were no good after the fire. The tension was gone.

We had lived on the farm all those years with no electricity, but it was coming our way. The families who lived in Foster City had had electricity for years. When power company representatives came and asked us if we wanted electricity, they didn't have to ask twice, but there was a lot for each customer to do to get it. First, we had to clear a right-of-way for the power lines Second, we had to use a certain amount of kilowatts. We were charged for them whether we used them or not, so we left our lights on all the time.

Some of the farmers had their own generators and didn't want electricity. They were satisfied with what they had.

We had to wire our house and the outbuildings since the power company only brought the power to our door. The rest was up to us. We helped Dad with the job, and it was harder than we thought it would be. We learned to work with hot wires so we would know if the lights worked.

One of the first things we got was an electric pump for the well, so we didn't have to depend on the windmill anymore, which was a great relief We don't notice the wind until we have to depend on it. When the wind didn't blow, we had to pump water by hand. When the wind blew too hard, we had to disconnect the windmill; otherwise, it would tear up the pump. It was nice to just turn the switch off or on at the pump and to not have to wait for the wind or fight it. In the winter, however, it was so cold the pump shaft would freeze. We had to put salt around it many times. The freezing weather would snap the arms on the pump.

We never did get a phone or an indoor bathroom. The most welcome item was the electric iron. Before we had it, our iron had to be heated on the stove. Once hot, we had to iron clothes as quickly as possible, before the iron cooled, which was all of fifteen minutes. We didn't have permanent press fabric, so we ironed everything. Before I got used to regulating the electric iron, I put a lot of brown spots on my clothes. I had to wear a sweater on the warmest days to cover a scorched spot or two on my blouse.

As we graduated from high school, we left home. When older children left, the younger children moved up the ladder. I guess it was like getting a promotion in a funny sort of way, but we had to take over more and more of the responsibilities. Even when I had the run of the house, I didn't like it. I was still compared to Marion, Anna, and Ruthie, which didn't help any. It was one of the reasons I didn't put much effort into my cooking and other household chores.

Running water was the next improvement on the agenda. First, we had to dig a ditch from the pump to the house, which was about fifty feet or so, and the ditch had to be six feet deep to get below the freeze line. We dug the ditch, laid the pipe into the basement, and put a line up to the sink in the kitchen. Since we had no septic tank, we put a bucket under the sink to catch the used water. When the bucket was full, we carried it out. I can't number the times the bucket overflowed and flooded the kitchen. It was another mess to clean up.

I began my last year in school, and I finally got my turn to learn to drive. I was seventeen when Wally and I got our licenses. It was an election year, and the sheriff needed all the votes he could get. There was no way we would fail the tests and not get our licenses. The driving test was easy. In fact, it was a snap. The sheriff wanted Dad's vote.

After a few years, Johnny came home from the army. He had served for two years in Germany. He stayed home for a while before he went to Waukegan to work.

Johnny always shared what he had, and I think that attribute made him stand out as a brother and as a person. He bought a new Chevy, and he would let me drive it, but I drove Dad's pickup truck most of the time. It was green and had a four-speed transmission. Driving wasn't a serious matter to me, which was the wrong way to feel about it even back then. Like most teenagers, speed was the big thing with me.

Then Dad bought an old red truck, which I drove into the woods when Dad and Wally worked there. My job was to drive; it was the easiest job. One day, I was on my way to the woods. Speeding was one of my biggest driving problems. There were a few sharp turns on the road. I knew it, and I should have slowed down, but didn't. I missed the turn and the bridge and headed toward the river. I got stuck in the river bank, which was just as bad as going into the river. Before I could walk to where Dad and Wally were working, I tried to figure out just what to tell Dad. In the meantime, the milkman came by and saw the truck on the river bank. He stopped and yelled at Dad, asking if he could help. Dad didn't know what he was talking about and came around the bend to see what was wrong. The milkman made such a joke that by the time we got the truck out of the river bank and had a cup of coffee, Dad was settled down a bit, but it was a silent afternoon. When an incident like that happened, I always took a few minutes to thank God that it wasn't any worse. I didn't get hurt, nor did I hurt anyone else. I knew I should think before I did, not the other way around.

One day, on the way home from town, I hit a dog. He wasn't hurt seriously, but I knew I couldn't leave him by the side of the road because he would die. I carefully picked him up and took him to his owner. We knew everybody in town, as well as their dogs. I knocked on the door, feeling good about doing the right thing. I told the dog's owner I was sorry for hitting her dog, even when it wasn't my fault, but when she saw the dog, she didn't even stop to check him out. She just grabbed him out of my arms and started bawling me out for what seemed like an eternity. When her husband heard the noise, he came into the kitchen. He shut her up in a minute and thanked me for caring for the dog. Despite the treatment I received. I would do the same thing if such an incident were to happen again.

During my senior year, my class was in the business of raising money, this time for ourselves. The money was for skip day and the only trip the class got to take. We were going to make the trip a good one, and that's what we did.

In October, we put on another play, Darling Brats. It, too, was a lot of fun to do and a lot of work. The play was a great success. Most events were. The town's people came out in full support of all school functions. If that tradition were in place today, the schools wouldn't want for anything.

In the spring, we had our annual carnival, which was a time-consuming project for the whole class. We went around to all the businesses in Foster City, Felch, and Iron Mountain. We collected a lot of donations for a wonderful evening and a door prize. We were set for a great trip to Chicago.

Then came the time I learned the hard way how to drive up a hill. Hills were bad enough in the summer, but in the winter, covered with the snow and ice, they were a different story. I had to go like crazy at the bottom of the hill to get enough momentum to carry me to the top. If I hit a slippery spot, I had to try again. One day, I was going up the hill with the truck. About halfway up, the wheels began to spin. A snow chain came loose and hit the brake line. All the fluid drained out, and I was without brakes. Down the hill I went, backward, gaining speed. I reached the bottom of the hill, saw no cars on the highway, and went across it in order to hit a snowbank to stop.

The next thing was to get the truck fixed. I drove the truck without brakes, through town, and down to the school garage for Steve to fix it. He was one of our bus drivers during the day, and when he wasn't driving, he was a mechanic for the school and for himself. He fixed the truck, and he didn't charge me for anything but the fluid. This incident happened a few more times before winter passed. I always got the truck fixed before Dad got home, but after all that time, Steve had told Dad. Dad never said a word.

One of my jobs was to take grains to Nurse Carlson so her husband could grind it into feed for the cattle. He was the only person in town with a mill. When it came time to pay, we would give him the money. If he needed to make a change, he would walk around the farm, and in about twenty minutes or so he would return with the money. A few times I tried to follow him, but he realized what I was doing, and he told me to go back to the truck. Mr. Carlson had money stashed all over the farm. No one knew where he kept it. When he and his wife passed away, their boys came to settle things. They dug all over the farm, but they didn't find much, if anything at all. Mr. Carlson had gone through the Great Depression, and I suppose that was his reason for not trusting banks.

Like most kids, I wanted to be part of the group at school. When offered a cigarette, I took it. I had no money to buy cigarettes, and I sure couldn't continue to borrow from the girls. Dad would buy a carton of

119

cigarettes at a time, and I would open the back and put in an empty pack stuffed with paper. When the carton was about empty, I would take out the empty pack and save it for the next time. The fact that I was stealing from Dad bothered me, however, and I really didn't like to smoke. So, after a while, I decided smoking wasn't worth the effort. If smoking was the way to be part of the gang, I didn't need it. It gave me a good feeling to stop smoking.

May came, and on the seventh, we boarded the Greyhound bus and headed for Chicago. We had looked forward to this day for months. We stopped in Milwaukee for a few hours, then we continued to the Conrad Hilton. There was nothing like staying in the fanciest place in town. We had enough money for skip day, and we had received some pocket money.

The first night, we all went to our first big league baseball game. As I sat there, I couldn't help but feel like someone special. Just being there for the first time made me feel special. The White Sox were playing the New York Yankees who wore their pinstriped uniforms. Casey Stengels was at the helm and the White Sox won. When we returned to the hotel, we sat up half the night talking and telling jokes.

The next day, we toured the city. We even went to skid row. I couldn't believe people lived through the winter on the streets like they did. Through the years, I wondered how many had died without anyone knowing or caring. I understood that some people couldn't help their circumstances, but a lot of them could have tried to make it out of skid row.

Of course, we couldn't go to the city without shopping. We went to Gimbles, which took in a whole city block. We had so much to look at, but I didn't buy much.

The next evening, we went to the Chicago Openair Ballroom. At that time, it was one of the finest establishments in Chicago. It was beautiful. It had a glass ceiling through which we could see the stars and we heard a live band. I enjoyed listening to the music even if I didn't dance. Being there was a treat in itself.

Early the next morning, we boarded the bus and headed north. We didn't have much in our pockets, but we had lots of memories, something we could take with us for the rest of our lives. No one could rob us of our memories.

With only a few weeks of school left, we were honored at our local churches. Each student attended the church of his or her choice for the baccalaureate service. There were four students attending the Swedish Covenant Church. Dressed in our gowns and caps, we marched down the aisle of the church and sat in the front row. The sermon was about our step into adulthood and the life that lay before us. The minister told us to take God with us, and He would keep us safe. Sure enough, through the years, God has taken care of me and blessed me in so many ways.

The last event was graduation night, and night of all nights. We would never turn back again, Graduation was the end of our school years. Some of us would never see each other again. That night, on stage for the last time, I felt emptiness as I listened to the speaker and as we received our long awaited diplomas, which indicated the end of that part of our lives. I returned home, and a little party was held in my honor. I felt good about my accomplishments, though they were few.

I was about to start a new phase of life. I stayed home through the summer to help Dad and Wally. Then, later in the fall, I ventured to Milwaukee to look for work.

During that time, our chickens weren't laying, so we bought eggs from Nurse Carlson. She loved to visit, no matter what time of day or night, and she wanted her visitors to stay and talk for a long time. It was hard getting away from her. One night when I had to go for eggs and didn't have a lot of time to visit, I decided to tell her a lie. I told her I had a cake in the oven, so I couldn't stay long. That was the worst thing I could have said. She began to tell me the dangers of leaving something like that. She told me how irresponsible I was. Of course, I couldn't tell her the truth, so I just sat and took it. When I had time, I liked to visit with her. She was a very interesting woman.

Felch High School, 1950s

Our Grandparents pictures

Chapter Nine
Stepping Out on My Own

Now that I had completed my schooling, I was about to step out on my own. I had a lot of big ideas, but they would change, and for everyone I altered, another took its place. We all have goals and dreams; otherwise, why do we strive?

I also found out that if I really wanted something, I could have it. Now that I look back years later, I did and got just about everything I really wanted. Some things were hard to come by; others were easy. The harder something was to accomplish, the more it meant to me. As we all know, things don't come easy. If they did, would they be worth it? I'm not so sure.

Moving away was a big decision for me. Where would I go to work? I had no experience. I had worked during high school, but only on the farm, and who wanted a farmhand?

There were no jobs in Foster City except farming, logging, or getting married, and those options were out of the question. I did a lot of praying and talked my concerns over with Marion. She always gave good advice, and I listened, even if I didn't agree. She was usually right. She never acted as though she were better than I. She promised she would pray for me, and she did through the years. There were times when I knew someone was looking out for me.

Then came another fall. I decided to go to Milwaukee to look for work. I knew it was a big step, but I had no idea how big. There were other girls from our area who worked there, so at least I knew someone.

In November I boarded the midnight train and headed for the city. Anna worked in Niagara, and she took me to the train. I had so many mixed feelings. I had a suitcase, and I had twenty dollars in my pocket. The money wasn't much, but it was enough to get me started during the 1950s. On the long ride through the night, the girls slept, but I didn't. I was wide-awake. So many things were rushing through my mind.

The train pulled into the station in downtown Milwaukee. I stepped off the train into the brisk, cool air, and I couldn't believe I was really there and on my own at last. My first task was to find a place to live; the second, to find a job. I sat down to a breakfast in a little café around the corner from the station, and I bought a newspaper. I couldn't believe the size of it. Our little paper back home had twenty pages at most. This paper had thirty pages of want ads alone. I knew I would find something I could do. I looked at the many pages of apartments for rent, but the prices! I couldn't believe the prices. I am not sure what I expected, but I knew there had to be something in my price range. I was beginning to face reality. The situation was not what I had expected, but I wasn't about to turn back. I knew no one would think less of me if I did go home, but I wouldn't.

In Foster City, when there wasn't a woman to cook and run the house, the youngest girl was expected to do so, and therefore, give up her future for her family. I was glad Dad didn't expect me to do that. He and I had spoken of it the last summer I was home. He never told me when to leave or what to do with my life. He just wanted me to be a good citizen and to stay out of trouble, which we had all done through the years. Now I am beginning to appreciate my upbringing, even if I hadn't during my youth. It was paying off. Dad could be really proud of the job he had done in rearing us kids. I am sure it was harder on him than it was on us through those years.

I began to walk the streets to find a place to hang my hat. I looked at many apartments, but there were few in my price range. Looking for a place to stay turned out to be a full day's job, but I finally found a boarding house for ten dollars a week. I felt good because I still had a few dollars in my pocket. The place wasn't much, but it was good enough until I got a job, which was my next step.

The house was a two-story building, almost in the center of town, so I was close to everything. It had three bedrooms upstairs and four down. It had a kitchen, and there was a phone in the hallway. There were about twenty-five girls staying there. I shared a bedroom with two of them. I didn't get to know them very well since I stayed to myself most of the time. We shared the kitchen. I didn't buy anything to put into the refrigerator. The other girls always seemed to fight over everything, and I wanted no part of it. I went around the corner to a café and ate my meals, which weren't many, until I got a job. I was so bashful I wouldn't change clothes in the bedroom if one of the girls were there. I was there to sleep; otherwise, I was job hunting or visiting the girls from Foster City.

The lady who ran to the boarding house was very understanding. She helped me to build my confidence while I looked for a job. I also noticed people didn't care where I came from or what my last name might be. It wasn't like Foster City where being a Swanson meant something. I liked it better that way. Now what I did with my life was up to me, and I wouldn't feel sorry for myself. I would go out there and get a job. I had mixed feelings from time to time, since I had only a few dollars in my pocket. I needed to go to work quickly!

The next morning, I began the job hunt. The experience was new to me. It wasn't like going to a farmer back home and asking for a job picking potatoes. I had never filled out an application for employment from the farmers. I just asked, and they said yes or no, and that was all there was to it. The first few days, I filled out applications, and I began to be discouraged, but I didn't give up. I wasn't about to go home. I kept going until I found a job.

I knew how to work since I had done it all through the years, but this was my first real job. On Thursday I went to the John Oster Manufacturing Company, and later I was called to go to work. I was happy. I didn't have a car, so I boarded the bus during the weekend and rode out to the plant so I would know the way.

The next morning, I was excited about finding my first job, but I wouldn't have a paycheck for two weeks, and I had only a few dollars left. I did a lot of studying the Bible and praying. As I had become older, God had become more real to me. At times like these, I had no one else to whom I could turn, and, of course, there was no one better I could have picked.

Work was interesting. There was a lot to learn. Speed was the most important skill on the assembly line. It was like being on a team. There were nine girls, so I had to learn in a hurry, and since it was my first job, it wasn't easy. There was an old, German lady, and she was forever on my case for the first few months. The other girls understood since they had all gone through the same initiation, including the German. She was money hungry, and it was awful working with her, even when I got up to speed with the rest of the girls.

One day, Doris, who later became my friend, told me not to worry because the German woman treated everybody like that, regardless of who they were. I was told not to take it personally, but it was hard not to. As time went on, I, too, laughed at her attitude towards everybody. She acted as if there were no one like herself.

I found out Doris stuck up for all the new kids on the block. That's when I decided I would stick to myself because there wouldn't always be a Doris around, and that's when my situation started to change. I believe we all have that drive, and when it surfaces, we need it. It's like added energy. I was really learning a lot about myself and how to survive in the big city. If I didn't take care of myself, who would?

As time went on, I wanted to live by myself. In the boarding house, I had no privacy. I was living with strangers.

I left my problem with God, and, lo and behold, life turned out a lot better when He took over. If God didn't take my problem, I took it back and tried to take care of it on my own, but, as we all know, that tactic doesn't work either.

Then came my first paycheck. I couldn't believe it was all my own. Since I had not learned to manage money, of course I blew my first few paychecks, and a lot more since. I believed in paying my bills, but saving was the farthest thing from my mind at the time. The landlady had agreed to wait for me to pay my back rent with my first check. I paid for it, then I went downtown and blew the rest. It was good I was paid weekly; otherwise, I wouldn't have made it through those first few months.

After a few weeks of living at the boarding house, I went looking for a new place to live. I found an apartment for ten dollars a week. It wasn't the best in town, but it was mine, and at last I was alone. The building was an old house that had been converted into apartments. The apartments had high ceilings, and they were badly in need of a painting job. There were three apartments on the first floor and two on the second. We had to share the bathroom, but I didn't mind. There was a big porch in front of the building, and we would sit out in the summer evenings and visit. That's when I began to meet the other tenants.

By this time, I had begun to be more outgoing, but I still had a long way to go. Things weren't the same anymore, but life went on, and there was no turning back.

I was still able to enjoy home for the Christmas holidays since the plant closed for two weeks. It was like taking a vacation, and I could see I had started to change. It wasn't my home anymore. I was still welcome, but once we are out on our own, it isn't quite the same.

Then I went back to work on the assembly line. By this time, I could keep up with the best of them. Two other girls from Foster City worked at the plant, which made it easier for me. We all need friends, and I was no different.

I started to make friends at work and at the apartment building, where the Knott family also lived. The Knott family turned out to be my best friends. They were so friendly, and they had me for dinner many times. They had four boys, and I baby-sat for them. Eddie and Darlene came from a small town like mine, so we had a lot in common. They were down-to-earth, nice people. We have kept in touch all these years. When they went to the Wisconsin Dells to visit their families, they invited me along, and we had so much fun. They treated me like one of their family.

I also needed a church, and that was my biggest problem. I went to a lot of them, but there was always something missing. At home I had enjoyed going to church and taking part in activities. I soon discovered there was a difference between religion and being a Christian. Those first years, I met Christians who had never stepped foot in a church. I'm not saying this lifestyle is right or wrong, so don't misunderstand. There are a lot of Christians in church. I attended as many as ten or twelve churches, but I just couldn't get used to their thinking. Part of the difficulty was mine. I wanted my church to be like the church in Foster City, so I didn't attend except when I went home on weekends, which was nearly every week.

I was asked to be on the company's bowling team. I had never picked up a bowling ball. That weekend. I bowled until my arms were sore, and I got the hang of it. I didn't know how to keep score, but that wasn't important to me since I could learn as time passed. No one will ever know how nervous I was that first night, but once I started bowling, I found out there were other bowlers no better than I. I was part of something, and that was a start for me. I bowled for the next three years I worked there.

During my third year, I was invited to go to a bowling tournament and, of course, I didn't have to be asked a second time. We even got to go out of town. The company put us up in a hotel, and I got my first trophy. It wasn't much for most folks, but to me, it was the best thing I had gotten in years. I was so proud. I had gotten it for something I had done and without someone telling me I should have done it like Marion, Anna, or Ruthie.

I enjoyed watching the Milwaukee Braves, whether on local TV or at the ballpark. In 1956, the Braves won the World Series, and the town went wild. People tore it up, and I mean that literally. They broke store windows downtown, burned taxi cabs, and destroyed whatever else they could get their hands on. It took days to clean up the mess, but we were all so happy the Braves had won, I guess we overlooked that part.

Then came the day I received the news that my sister, Marion, had suffered a stroke. She was in the hospital for a long time, so every weekend I went home to see her. When she came home from the hospital, someone had to be with her all the time, which created a problem. Kenneth had to work, and the rest of the family had good jobs. I, however, had nothing special going on, and there were rumors of a layoff at the company. So, I went into the office and asked if I could be one of the first workers to be laid off. I told my employers about Marion, and they were willing to go along with me. Within weeks, I was laid off.

I packed my few belongings and went to Foster City. I was more than glad to stay with Marion and her two oldest children, Judy and Gordy. The youngest, Gary, stayed with Kenneth's parents. I was able to create unemployment, so I had pocket money, which was all I needed back then.

Marion stayed with us when she first came home, but while she was in the hospital, we took turns staying with her so rails wouldn't have to be put on her bed. She didn't want them. We had to help her turn in bed when she wanted to turn. She had to take three or four shots a day, so one can imagine how sore she got after a month or so. I stayed at the hospital once in a while, but mostly Kenneth and Anna stayed. Marion had always been there when any of us needed her

Marion came home after a few months. She had to learn to talk, and she stuttered a lot. For a long time, she didn't speak unless she had to. She had to learn to write again, too, and she'd had the best handwriting of any of us. Now her handwriting was no better than mine. Marion worked hard to bring her writing and reading back to normal. The best thing for me was being able to do something for her. I became closer to her, and it was now my time to pray for her instead of the other way around.

A few months later, Marion was well enough to go home, but she had been away from Gary for three or four months, and he hardly remembered her. It took a while for him to get used to her, which hurt her, but it was no one's fault. It was just the way things were. It wasn't long, however, before they were a family again, once they all got into their own house. Judy was in school, so I took her there every day. Gordy went with me. I enjoyed the kids. We had a lot of good times, and they got away with a lot when staying with me.

It was lonesome without Marion, but I knew it was time to move on. Summer was coming, and I was still unemployed. Then, Anna asked me if I wanted to go on vacation for a week with her and with a friend of her's, Sue. Of course, I was more than happy to go. We went to Copper Country, which is about one hundred miles north of Foster City. It was one of the most beautiful places I have ever seen, and I have been to a lot of places during my lifetime. We rented a cabin for a week and had a great time.

One of the most spectacular places where the Kitch-it-ki-pi Springs. They were so clear and calm they looked like a mirror. They were located near the city of Manistique. We rode in a glass-bottom boat, and we could see down a hundred feet or more into the water. It was amazing how clear the water was. I often wonder if it is still that clear or if man has spoiled it, too. Of course, this location was connected to the Indians, and there were still plenty of signs of the once proud people of that area.

We spent a day at Macinac Island, where there were no motorized vehicles except for a fire truck and an ambulance. We had to travel by boat to get to the island. We took the earliest boat from the mainland, so we had a full day before us. We rented bicycles in the morning. It was fun riding around without watching for cars, but there were a lot of horse-drawn carriages. After returning the bicycles, we took a ride on one of them. It was great, and the driver told us about the island and its history. The restaurants were also great, and there was no shortage of gift shops.

We wanted to go completely around the island, and bicycles wouldn't do, so we rented horses. People deciding to make this trip shouldn't tell the stable owners they can ride, even if they are good riders. They will be given an animal according to their riding talents. We said we could ride like champs, so we were given horses with minds of their own and the strength to go with them. Once we mounted, they were like racehorses. They left the gate and didn't stop running until we returned a few hours later. They took off around the island like there was no tomorrow. They either stopped, or they ran all out. When we brought them back, they were sweating and foamy. Those who know anything about horses, know horses are not supposed to get that way, but we had no choice. Our excuses didn't seem to matter to the owner. He told us about their condition in no uncertain terms. We were just glad to get off those horses Thank God they had saddles, so we had been able to hang on.

Our next venture was to the Soo Locks. It's hard to imagine how big they are. They are the busiest locks in the world. We rode a tour boat and went in with an ocean liner. It was like being a speck in the corner of a sink. It was interesting how the workers raised and lowered the water in each lock, a work of art for whoever designed and built them. Half the locks belong to Canada, but we couldn't tell. They looked the same.

We also took in the pictured rocks, which consisted of rock formations of different shapes and sizes. It was about a two-hour cruise and a lot of fun. We met many vacationers. We did several activities that week, and time seemed to just fly by. When having fun, it is always that way.

We also went to Tahquanemon Falls. The Indian name for the place is "Land of Hiawatha." most of the sites up our way were named after the Indians. We had a picnic there and watched the falls. There is half a dozen or so in the area, and they are all different in their own way. The place is hard to describe, because to most people, waterfalls are waterfalls, and that's all there is to it.

We hiked to the top of the Porcupine Mountains. It took us a few hours to get there, but the view was magnificent. We ate everywhere we went, and that, too, was fun. We didn't have to cook or do the dishes.

Before we knew it, we were headed out of the Copper Country and back to Foster City, but the three of us had many memories for the rest of our lives, which is the way friendships are born and kept through the years. Even if we don't see each other often, we still have a spot in our hearts for each other.

Back home, I got restless again, and I was called back to work after five or six months. I was glad to get back to work, even if it was on the assembly line. I missed my friends in Milwaukee. I enjoyed sitting around visiting during our breaks and being on the bowling team, etc. I also enjoyed sitting out in the evening at the old apartment building. I liked visiting with all the different kinds of folks. They were very interested in their own sort of way.

After a week or so, I was asked if I would be interested in moving into the shipping department. I couldn't wait to get off the assembly line. In the shipping department, we had to pack and ship the various items, so every day was different, but I soon tired of that job, and I knew I would have to move on. But to where? That was the big question. Since I didn't have a trade, where to go and what do to was the problem.

Then I got the idea that I needed and wanted a car, which turned out to be one of my biggest mistakes. Of course, being young and wanting to do it, that is exactly what I did.

I bought a used, 1950 Mercury, and it was well used. I didn't know anything about car dealers and how they talk people into buying things they really don't need, which is what one did to me.

Still, the car was all mine, mine and the finance company's, I should say, and I had bought someone else's troubles. Within a few months, I had a great deal of trouble. I kept the car for a year or so, then I traded it for another used car. During the winter, because of the snow in the city, each night I had to park the car on a different side of the street on even numbered days so the odd numbered side of the street could be cleaned. Each night I had to make sure I was on the correct side of the street.

I had plenty of friends, a carload all the time. They weren't the same people who helped me when I first came to the city. These friends came out of the woodwork for a free ride. They never volunteered to buy gas, nor did they give me a few bucks for fuel. They knew, as well as I did, that I could not operate a car without those good old greenbacks. After a while, I asked them for money for gas, and, to my surprise, they all found a different means of transportation. I guess they found another sucker because I am sure I wasn't the only one in the city. I didn't have to ask my old friends for money; they paid their own way.

I began to hate going to work. If it weren't for the paycheck, I wouldn't have stayed as long as I did. I knew a person shouldn't work at something he or she hates because life is so short, it isn't worth it. So, I started looking for something else. I wanted to travel, so what better place than the armed forces? I joined in a few days.

I took the written test without trouble. I didn't get the highest score, but it was good enough. My weight was the problem. I had to lose thirty pounds or so to get in; otherwise, I was in good health.

The recruiting officer set up an appointment the following week with a doctor who could help me to lose weight. He said I couldn't do it in thirty days, but I was determined. First of all, I had to discipline myself. I drank a lot of coffee, took vitamins, and did a lot of exercises. I lost the weight in thirty days, just as I said I would.

134

I gave two weeks' notice to the company where I worked, and I was surprised that my coworkers thought enough of me to give me a cake and gifts. I began to understand that people cared, no matter what was said.

When I told my dad, he didn't say much, but he didn't like it. I could tell by his face. After a week at home and a handshake, I was once again on my way. I didn't have a party like Johnny had when he went into the army, but I didn't expect one. Johnny had been drafted. I had volunteered, but the biggest reason was because I was a woman. Nice girls didn't do a thing like that; however, if a woman is going to be a bad girl, she will be one, regard-less of where she lives or what she does.

Marion and I talked about it, and she said, "Do what you want to do, not what someone else wants, as long as you're not hurting anyone in the process." She would continue to pray for me, and that was a good feeling of relief.

On August 3, 1958, I signed on the dotted line, and I was sworn in. I was on my way to a new life, and I was looking forward to it. Before I went into the service. I went on a last trip to the Dells with the Knott family. They supported me through my decision, and they treated me like family. I missed going to the farm.

I had to sell my car, which I sold to friends who took me to the cleaner's. They never got the title changed, nor did they make the last payments. Creditors caught up with me later, and I had to make the final payments. I never heard from those people again. I guess they weren't as good of friends as I had thought. I had learned a lesson, or I hoped I had.

I was ready to board the plane to Texas to start my military career. I felt sad to leave my friends and relatives, but I looked forward to the change, and a change it was!

Tahquanemon Falls

Indian Rock

The Knott Family

Iris and Me

1956, My family

CHAPTER TEN
MY AIR FORCE YEARS

I boarded a train for Milwaukee after a short visit with friends and family. I began to ponder the events of the last few days and wondered if I had made a mistake. Many people had given their opinions, mostly against my decision to join the air force. They thought I would become a tramp or gay. There was no middle of the road as far as they were concerned.

Thanks to God and to the many prayers and concerns of my family and friends, I was safe, as I knew I would be if I followed what I was taught as a child and while growing up. I now understood what family ties really meant.

I took my first plane ride and received my first meal flying thousands of feet above the clouds. It was a new and exciting experience. Today, the ride would not be something to brag about, but at that time it was. We landed in Texas, at the San Antonio Airport. My sitting back and letting stewardesses wait on me was about to come to an abrupt halt. For the next eight weeks nobody, and I mean nobody, would wait for me.

I deboarded the plane. There was a taxi and a big blue bus with the words "U.S. Air Force" written across the side in bold letters. I couldn't miss it.

When we arrived at Lackland Air Force Base, we met a lot of military personnel, who would become our mothers, fathers, and everything between. They began by telling us how worthless we were, and at times I felt that way. This was one time I felt like saying something, but I kept my mouth shut. The less said, the better off I would be.

Life was different than the recruiting officer had led me to believe. He had painted a pretty picture. Of course, people can't believe everything recruiting officers say, and if they believe half, they believe too much.

We traded our civilian clothes for the standard blue uniforms and com-bat boots. I realized I was in the service for the next three years. I was determined to make it and make it I did.

We arrived at LAFB at about 11:00 P.M., or as they say twenty-three hundred hours. We were assigned to our barracks, four girls to a room. It wasn't like the men's army where the whole building is one room. I had good roommates. We used to lay on our bunks and talk away the hours as if we didn't have anything else to do. We had all come from different parts of the country, so at first, we didn't have much in common, but it was nice sharing our lives with each other. In Milwaukee, I met people from different backgrounds, but most had come from the same general area, within one hundred miles of each other.

In basic training, we came from all fifty states and then some. The first thing I noticed was the general outlook on life. Some didn't care what they did or said. Others were running from something, their home life, a love affair, etc. sooner or later, however, our troubles catch up with us. The girls for whom I felt sorry were those who had never been out on their own before coming into the service. They couldn't handle life's problems without their parents looking over their shoulders for guidance. They got into trouble in a hurry because they couldn't cope with that way of life. I was twenty-one years old and had been on my own for a few years, so I was more grown up the most.

I sat around and listened to some of the stories the girls talked about men they had dated and slept with. I was grown up in a lot of ways but not in the area. If I had tried to tell the story, it would have been so boring, no one would listen, so -I listened instead.

There was nothing like basic training, and there never would be again. Our day started at 4:00 A.M. with a wakeup call. We dressed in a few minutes and went out on the sidewalk in formation. Then we went to the mess hall for breakfast. I had a hard time getting used to eating breakfast at that hour in the morning. I thought it was the middle of the night. I also learned to eat in a hurry and to not talk. I loved to visit, whether at mealtime or just sitting around the barracks, but after getting caught a time or two for talking at the table and having to stand at attention while the rest of the squadron ate, it didn't take me long to learn to keep my mouth shut. While in basic training, we didn't have to pull KP. The air force was the only branch of the service in which the guys did KP for us. With no snacking during the day, I looked forward to mealtime, and I enjoyed the food. I know that's hard to believe.

I thought a person could only be so clean, but the military had its own definition. When the inspecting officer came around, he flipped a quarter on our bunks, and if it didn't bounce, he made us redo our bunks over and over until it did. I always had trouble making my bunk satisfy the officers. They made sure no one was perfect, and they always found something wrong. There was no way to get around it. After making my bunk enough time, I got the idea to sleep on the floor and make the bunk once a week. It saved a lot of time.

We had a lot of night fire drills. Each of us would grab a blanket and run outside. One night, we had an unexpected fire drill. The whistle sounded, and we all jumped up. In my haste, I forgot to take the blanket off my bunk. Instead, I took the one I used for sleeping on the floor. While we stood outside, the officer in charge went inside the barracks to check the rooms before letting us back in. When she got to my bunk, she was quite upset, to say the least. I spent the rest of the night making and remaking my bed. I was never so glad to see the sun come up so I could go about the day's routine. I should have known better because I knew short cuts just don't pay, but I continued to try. This experience was just another night in the life of a trainee, and I learned to make my bed by the time my eight weeks were up.

We went to classes during the day to study military ways. There is only one way to do things in the air force, and the trainers did a good job of whipping us into shape in just eight weeks. I enjoyed the classes. They were very interesting, but they also gave us time to sit down and doze off a time or two. Not getting caught was the trick.

We had to march everywhere we went, always in a group. It was real togetherness! I hated marching because I had an awful time keeping in step. I always took bigger steps than most of the girls, so I was continuously out of step. Our drill sergeant was sure he could teach us to march, so he kept girls like me out at night on the parade field, and we marched until the wee hours of the morning. Believe it or not, I did get the hand of it, but it took a while.

We had to wear nylons with seams with our uniforms. For one parade, two of us didn't have nylons, much less ones with seams, so we drew lines down the back of our legs. Nobody knew the difference.

CQ (Charge of Quarters) was another job. The girl pulling CQ was in charge of the barracks and had to stay awake all night to keep an eye on things. She was a glorified babysitter. When an officer entered, she had to call the barracks for attention in respect for the officer's rank.

One day, I had pulled CQ, and an officer came into the barracks. So, like a good airman, I called the barracks to attention. He was a major. I then went about my business, and about an hour later another officer showed us at our door. Without thinking, I once again called attention. The only trouble was that the officer was only a first lieutenant. Of course, we all know that a major outranks a first lieutenant. This call to attention was a no-no because there was already a higher-ranking officer in the barracks. These people came around at all hours of the day or night just to catch us off guard, and they sure did! I had to pull CQ three nights in a row. I never made that mistake again. During the day, I had to go to my squadron, and by the third night I was so tired, but I kept going. I wasn't about to give them the satisfaction of breaking me.

Some of the girls could not adapt to the way of life, even if it was only for eight weeks. Some washed out, and others took ten to twelve weeks to complete their basic training. Others just wanted out and didn't even try to make it. Of course, they were discharged and sent home.

We didn't have much time for ourselves, only Saturday afternoons and Sundays. On Sundays, we went to the church of our choice. We had to go. On weekends, we did our laundry, wrote letters, etc. I was fortunate and received a lot of mail, but there were some who received no mail at all for the full eight weeks we were there.

Our uniforms were made from 100 percent cotton, and we had to starch and iron them daily. They were so full of starch, they were able to stand up by themselves! A lot of girls had never done laundry before, and some, I think, had never seen a washing machine before. So, a few of us tended to their uniforms for a price. We couldn't go anywhere anyway. I didn't really care about the job, but the money was good, and I just had to take advantage of a situation like that.

Then came the shining of shoes. That was a job of its own on weekends, and it was so time consuming. If we were careful, we could buff up shoes during the week and make them last to the weekend before we really had to polish them. I just didn't like to spit shine them, and that's all there was to it. Some of us got the idea we could let someone else do it, and we gave our shoes to a couple of Mexican boys. They were about twelve or thirteen years old, and they hung out around the base. They did a great job on our shoes in no time flat. One day, in formation, I was given special attention because my shoes were shining. I just stood there and took the praise since we didn't get much of that during basic training.

We also never squealed on anyone. Oh, there were a few who did, but before long, they had no friends. No one could trust or like them after that.

Then came the "Yes, ma'am," or the "No, ma'am," and the "Yes, sir," or "No, sir," along with saluting officers in respect for their rank. Sometimes, I swear, they paced themselves so we would have to salute twenty times. I think they got a kick out of it, especially in basic training. Even today I say, "Yes, sir," or "No, sir," and "Yes, ma'am," or "No, ma'am." It's hard to break the habit, yet I think this habit is a good one to get into because it shows respect for the people with whom you have to deal, even after basic training.

It seemed as if the only thing we ever did was clean and reclean. We had white-glove inspections, and if the inspection party came up with any dust while checking the barracks, we were in trouble again. They checked the blinds above the windows, our lockers, and our drawers. If anything was out of place, they dumped our drawers on our bunks and made us do them over. All of our things had to be rolled in a certain way. If they weren't, there were no excuses. If things weren't right in our lockers, they did the same thing, and if things didn't go right, we ended up with a real mess in our room.

At night, we played cards in the latrine because it was the only place with no window. No one could tell if the lights were on or not. I learned to play cards there, and I could win with the best of them. I enjoyed it, and even today I enjoy playing cards.

1959, Basic Training, Lackland AFB

1960, Firepower Demo. Eglin AFB

Then it got to the point where we would see how much we could get away with. It became a game, and it helped to pass the time. We had a few laughs at the same time, too.

The only good thing that came out of this experience was that I lost twenty pounds and was in tiptop shape when the eight weeks were over. We couldn't snack between meals, which helped. I felt good about myself and how I looked.

Then we completed the basics. We had only known each other for eight weeks, but we had gotten to know each other well and had become good friends. On graduation day, there was a parade in our honor, and the top brass made speeches to let us know we had completed our first step in military life (the hardest step). Now we were ready to move on, and we looked forward to it.

We waited for orders. Some of us weren't so lucky and were stationed at LAFB. Others moved on to more schooling or to permanent assignments. We said our good-byes and went our separate ways with great anticipation about the future.

My heart was heavy because I knew we would never see each other again; however, some of us have kept in touch through the years. Our friendships have grown, and our paths have crossed since then.

We got our orders and huge paychecks of eighty-seven dollars per month, along with our travel pay. Many girls took fifteen days leave, but I saved my furlough until Christmas. I wanted to be home for the holidays. I had never missed Christmas at home.

Some of the girls were sent to a school of one kind or another. I was sent to my first and only assignment for the air force. I went to Eglin Air Force Base in Florida, along with three other girls. None of us were close friends, but that's how it goes. We traveled by train, so we were able to see the scenery through the deep South. I was excited to see places I had only read about.

I had never been prejudiced against anyone. While growing up in Michigan, there was nothing to be prejudiced about. We were all white folks, mostly Swedes. I really can't say whether I would have been prejudiced or not, but in the South, a lot of people were prejudiced and still are. Maybe they have a right to be. Who knows? Some things people can't change overnight.

I didn't notice any prejudice in the air force, as I looked back, although I'm sure there was some in the military, but since I wasn't looking for it, I didn't notice it.

While traveling by train, there were some stops along the way where we could get off and go into the train depot to walk around a little. We were on the last leg of the trip and going through Mississippi when we stopped for an hour. We decided to check out the depot and have something to eat. Food was a lot cheaper in the depots than it was on the train. I had to use the restroom, and I was in a hurry. I saw the restroom for women and went in. To my surprise, it was a women's restroom, all right, but it was for colored people. I hadn't noticed the sign on the door. Once inside, it was too late. A biz-colored gal picked me up from the floor and slammed me against the wall. I'm not a small person, but I didn't say a word, and I didn't have to go to the bathroom after that. When she let me down. I understood fully what was going on in the South. She didn't want me in her restroom any more than whites wanted her in theirs. This experience struck me through the years. Even if we want to be the same, we're not.

"We finally made it to Florida. Eglin looked good to me. It was a big place, and it was my first and only duty assignment during my three years in the air force. It took me awhile to get settled and used to my new way of life. This Assignment was an altogether different experience from basic training. There asse no more early formations, but we did have parades and such. I didn't have a car, nor did I buy one while I was in the air force. Everything was within walking distance.

There were only two of us in a room, and I had a great roommate, Rose, but we were as different as day and night. We never saw much of each other, except in passing. She had her friends, and I had mine. On the other hand, she was very helpful in showing me the ins and outs of military life, such as it was. I was quickly becoming more outgoing. I had no choice, and it didn't take me long to figure out who was who.

During my first assignment, I was a clerk. I was sent to a typing class, which included air force style procedures. It wasn't the assignment I wanted, but I had no choice. There were a lot of jobs women couldn't get into, so we took what we got.

I worked in a supply unit. The people were great, and a good NCO was in charge. Everyone on base was our friend because we had access to supplies, and we had much bargaining power.

As the new kid on the block, my coworkers played jokes on me to see if I could take it. When I proved I could, I soon became one of the groups. I knew of people who did not fit in. All the units played these sorts of tricks to break in new personnel.

One trick that stands out in my mind was the time the guys decided to pit me against Betty. We were the only two girls in the unit, and the guys liked to play tricks on us. When I first got to EAFB, the basketball season had just started. Betty was on the same team I was hoping to join. When Betty returned to work from out of town, the guys told her I had been with her boyfriend. She was jealous, and she showed it.

She wasted no time calling me on this matter. I wasn't sure what to do but I knew I had to stand up for myself. There was no one to stick up for me. I grew tired of her pushing me around, so when she started in again, I got up and went to her desk. I took off my jacket and asked her to step outside to fight it out. This response took her by surprise, and she decided against it. I am not sure what I would have done had she said okay. She was bigger than I, she had been there a lot longer, and she had more rank, but at that point, I didn't care. After that, we were on the same basketball team, and we became friends. I think she was pleased to see me make the team so she could keep an eye on me.

We didn't have a girls basketball team in high school, so I really had to work hard to make the team. Most of the girls had played in school. When I made the team, my dreams began to come true. I had gone to the gym regularly to practice so I could be sure of making the team.

The first year I signed up as a forward because I thought it would be more fun. The guards never got a chance to score like they do today, but in a few months, it dawned on me that I should have been a guard. I didn't play much, and I would have been a much better player as a guard. I switched over, but I wasted a whole season.

The game was different then. There were three guards and three forwards on each end of the floor. The guards couldn't shoot, and the players could only dribble once. Years later, the rules were changed, and we played the whole floor. There were five players from each team on the floor at that time.

We played in the army, navy, air force, and civilian teams. I always had a good time playing and traveling to other places. We were always treated like VIPs, and it was nice to be noticed. Many people came to watch us play.

We were flown to most of our games on the air force planes that had the old metal seats on each side and were cold in the winter! We wore our pajamas under our uniforms to keep warm, and to pass the time, we played cards on a table made up of our parachutes.

One time when we played at the navy base during Mardi Gras, there were about four or five teams housed at the base. We wanted to go to town, but one team couldn't go because the officer in charge wouldn't let them. So, they put the officer in a wall locker, turned the door to the wall, and went to town. The next morning was another matter. The whole team was sent back to their base.

Many civilian teams had no colored girls, and they wouldn't play with us until we got rid of ours, which we refused to do. The military wouldn't stand for it, nor would the team members. We just didn't play those teams.

We got much press coverage during basketball and softball season. Most of us were given nicknames, which I supposed goes along with sports. Since I had red hair, the natural thing was to call me "Red," and that nickname stuck with me through the years.

There was real competition between the different branches of the service. We played in military and civilian tournaments, and the more competitive, the better we liked it.

If we didn't win, the base commander wanted to know why. The officers were proud of us and wanted winning teams.

My softball years in the Air Force

I liked the travel, even if it was only for a few days at a time. We had fancy uniforms: one set was for away games, another for home games.

During this time, I learned much about myself. I was equal to anyone and had to take a backseat to no one. I gained spirit and was becoming competitive. I hated to lose, and even today I hate to lose. We all have a competitive spirit. We just need a reason to bring it out.

I believed in myself. My accomplishments were up to me. I wasn't afraid to make mistakes. When I did, I just tried harder.

We had to pull KP once a month at our permanent base. The holidays were coming up, and I needed money to go home. I pulled KP for other girls on weekends and made good money. No one cared who pulled KP or how often, just so there was somebody there at 3:00 A.M.

It was nice to be home for the holidays, even if it were for only a few days, but things were different. Wally and Carol had gotten married, and they were living with Dad on the farm. Things would never be the same there again. It wasn't anyone's fault, it was just how life went.

While growing up, all I ever heard about God was from the fire and brimstone perspective, but that view alone wasn't true. When I went to church on the base, I found out that person could smile, laugh, and live life to the fullest and still be a Christian. Through the years, God has closed many doors to me, but for every door He's closed, He's opened as many, if not more, and the ones He has opened were more than I expected.

After a successful basketball season, with the coming of spring, we looked forward to softball. Softball was more my game! I knew most of the rules, and I had played it before, even if it were in a cow pasture back home on Sunday afternoons or at the city park in Milwaukee a few years before.

To play softball was something I really wanted, so I went after it. I also found out that softball was like basketball; we played to win. We were decked out in our red and white uniforms, and we played the same teams as we did in basketball.

We won, but I suffered a few minor accidents. Playing first base was dangerous. Runners stepped on me for something to do. At that time, we wore steel cleats on our shoes. During the first few games, my legs were scratched up. It didn't take me long to change my way of playing. Sliding into home plate was exciting, especially when I was called safe, but, once, the catcher politely stepped on my leg and grinned. I was taken to the base emergency room for eight stitches and a chipped bone. I still have the scar; otherwise, I faired pretty well and got my shots in from time to time.

During one state tournament, we went to Key West, Florida, and finished in fourth place in the state. I guess that ranking wasn't too bad, but since we weren't first, it didn't make much difference where we finished in the standings. The tournament committees always furnished board, room, medical personnel, batboys, etc.

We had a great batboy. He kept the dugout clean and neat, and he had a wonderful personality, but he was good for nothing else. He stole from us blind. He didn't even leave us a dime. He took everything he could carry off, wallets, watches, etc. We were in Key West without a penny to our names. Thank God it didn't take the police long to find him, and he confessed, but we still had no money. He had already spent it. We did, however, get back our empty wallets and our watches. We lived through the ordeal and gained experience in the process.

I had been on the bowling team in Milwaukee a few years before, and I bowled for three years in the service. I was on the Demon team. There were only four bowlers on the team, and I carried an average of one hundred thirty, so I had a nice handicap. One year, we received a trophy for the highest game even when we did end up in last place. At this point, I was enjoying life and making some good friends.

I spent a year in the supply area, then I was transferred to the Boat Squadron as a clerk typist. The assignment was different than the one with the supply group. All I had done in the supply group was type forms and check supplies. In the Boat Squadron, I was more my own boss. I had an office and all, but I still had to type letters for the commander. The dictionary was my salvation, but like everything else, I learned after many mistakes. Some would be surprised at what I could do, but put in a situation like I was, I had no choice.

I dated, but no serious relationships developed. Then, a sergeant asked me out, but I didn't care for him. He wanted me to move in with him. I turned him down, and to my surprise, he said, "You won't get promoted, if you don't do what I want." Sure enough, he was right. I didn't get a promotion for months. My values had been instilled in me at an early age, and I intended to keep them. It cost me at times, but I stuck to them.

We played ball in different places, and once I met an air force photographer from Orlando AFB. He took many pictures, and we became good friends since neither of us wanted to get married. Later, we both married, but not each other. I lost dates because of my values, but I gained respect from others. So, it works both ways. People have to do what feels right to them and not let other people talk them into situations they don't want. They need to just say, "No."

After about six months on the Boat Squadron, I met the Kirkpatrick's. They were a great family. I was the only one in the office doing a job for a sergeant. I was still an airman, third class. Kirk became my supervisor, and he worked with me in supply. So, I already knew him and his family. He got me promoted in a few months since he was also on the promotion board.

His wife, Betty, was the type of person who stood out in a crowd and did her own thing. She didn't try to please everyone. They had two boys, Kord and Pat. I did a lot of babysitting while Betty was in the hospital and Kirk went to school at night. Pat was easygoing, or so I thought. Kord, on the other hand, was rough and tough. When he did something, everyone knew it. Pat could get Kord so mad. He could irritate him just sitting and watching TV, but if they were outside and someone started a fight with either of them, they stuck together like glue.

The Boat Squadron retrieved the missile heads for the 3208 Test Group, so we had seven or eight boats. We were like a family. We had parties and fishing trips, which I enjoyed very much. On weekends, we would get together and go deep-sea fishing or grabbing. We always had a good time.

I loved to sit out on the deck, even if I wasn't fishing. Of course, without fail, I got a nice sunburn. I never tan, regardless of what I did to prevent a burn. I ended up just wearing a shirt. I looked funny running around the deck and wearing a shirt. The rest of the group never had that trouble.

I liked to go deep-sea fishing because we always caught our limit. It wasn't like fishing when I was a kid. Back then, we went for months without catching anything. There were plenty of fish in the Gulf of Mexico, and when we caught our limit, we had a fish fry on the beach.

We also did a lot of grabb fishing which was fun, too. We would take the boat out to a sandbar when the tide was going out, and we would be grounded for a few hours. Once the tide was out, we all jumped over the side of the boat and caught as many grabbs, or clams, as possible before they could bury themselves in the sand. Once again, we headed back to the beach for a party. They were eating good food.

On the beach, we built a fire and cooked the grabbs or fish. We went as a group so we could sing and dance on the sand. We were all from the same unit, so it was like a family. We didn't always get along, but if someone else messed with anyone in our unit, it would cause a war.

Sometimes a group of us would get together and rent a boat and scuba gear from the base boat shop. We could rent the equipment for pennies a day. I didn't learn to scuba dive like most. I just put on the gear and jumped overboard. I was glad the water wasn't deep the first few times. The first fish I saw underwater looked like a whale. A turtle seemed like a monster. Everything was much bigger underwater. As a large person, I never felt good about my size, except at times like that when I had to wear added weight to stay at the bottom. What a joy.

I also enjoyed water-skiing. It was hard for me to get up the first few times, but once I got the hang of it, it was fun. I always wore a life jacket. Since the experience at Norway Lake years before, I never took chances when it came to the water. I could never ski on one foot or do other stunts like that. We all took turns driving the boat, and that was fun, too. I just enjoyed doing things with people.

We also drove go-carts. We went downtown and had a good time on Saturdays. We didn't drive in competition or anything. This activity, too, was just to see who was best. We raced among ourselves. It was an enjoyable afternoon.

We couldn't go anywhere in Florida without seeing stands along the road selling alligators. They were supposed to be the miniature ones. One selling alligators. road sent Anus's daughter, Roxanne, a couple of them, but they didn't remain small. They got bigger and bigger and grew to be six feet long. She ended up putting them in a bathtub and feeding them hamburger. I found out later that many people from the roadside stands raided the regular alligators' nests, got the eggs, and hatched them. After a few years, the law put

a stop to that practice. I enjoyed Florida, with its sandy beaches and nice weather. There was always something to do, but along with these advantages came the ugly side of Florida, hurricane season. Michigan didn't even have high winds, let alone hurricanes.

First came the high winds, with power to spore, then the destruction and floods. I've seen hurricanes totally destroy trailer parks and homes as if they were dollhouses. The storms took hours to pass. The only good news was the fact that we knew they were coming. We were warned of their approach, but we could only prepare so much, then hope.

In 1961, one of the worst storms took out orange groves as it passed. It was moving up the east coast, but suddenly it turned inland

and destroyed everything in its path. It was headed straight for us. First, we had to clear the flight line. All the planes were flown north to other bases. The planes wouldn't have stood a chance in those winds. Then we had to tie down everything and take in all the townspeople from around the base. Most of their homes and trailers would not survive the storm. We couldn't take a chance with their lives. The people were moved to the base since our buildings were made from bricks and could stand the wind pressure.

We gave our rooms to the people, like good troopers, and we worked around the clock to make them as comfortable as possible. Most of them were very cooperative. We read stories to the children and were glorified baby-sitters. We knew that some of the people would go home to nothing, so it was worthwhile helping them for a few days.

Besides housing the people, we had to feed them. It was a good thing the mess hall was just around the corner. We tied the kids together with rope and walked them to the mess hall. Some children got a kick out of it, others were scared.

The wind was bad, then the eye came. It was an eerie feeling because in the eye, there is no wind-none-and we knew that in a little while, there would be more wind and more destruction, After the storm passed came the cleaning up, but we were glad the storm was over, and everything was once again back to normal.

It seemed as if we slept for days after being up all the time. Since we had been busy, we had just kept going and had not noticed fatigue until the experience was over. Then we felt it.

I made a trip to Gonzales, Texas, with Windy to visit her family. They always treated me as if I were one of them. Windy's mother made the best meals. Their way of life was good old country living, just the way I liked it. We rode horses and went fishing. They always had something going on when I was there. We sat on the porch and talked for hours, sometimes until the sun came up in the morning. We slept out on the porch in the summer.

Everyone called me Red, including Windy's family. They had a western belt made for me with my name on it. I have cherished it through the years, along with many other gifts I have received. I think the gifts people make for me are worth a lot more than what they buy.

One weekend, a group of us went to Bellingrath Gardens, a beautiful estate dedicated to the memory of Bellingrath's wife. A lazy, flowing stream ran through the garden, and it contained every kind of flower imaginable. The most beautiful spot was the rose garden. I hadn't seen anything like it, except for the Rose Gardens in Shreveport, Louisiana. A hilltop mansion overlooked the garden as if to keep an eye on all its beauty.

I liked the dog races, too, but I wasn't much of a gambler. If I wagered ten dollars, I was doing well. I didn't win much. Sometimes we pooled our money and bet on a few dogs. Then we split the winnings. We were in the service and had little money. We were only rich for a few days after payday. By the end of the week, we were broke again, but, then again, I was never good at handling money anyway.

I always picked the dog who took a potty break before the race. I figured he would be lighter. He wouldn't have that little extra weight. It was a crazy idea, but it was the best I could come up with at the time. Now and then, a dog jumped on the fence, cut across the track, and waited for the rabbit on the other side. Once a dog did something like that, he never raced again.

It was time for me to reenlist or get out. I had a hard decision to make. The only decision I regret is that I didn't take advantage of the college education to which I was entitled. I decided to leave the air force and spent two weeks in Key Largo, Florida, with the Kirkparticks. Then I packed my belongings, boarded a bus, and headed north. I had been lucky to meet so many nice people; it was like home away from home.

I have never regretted the choice to serve in the U.S. Air Force. My memories are many more than I can write, but, as we all know, we can't write down all of our memories because if we did, we would fill volumes instead of one book.

God always looked out for me, even when I thought I didn't need Him that much. Marion's prayers kept me out of trouble. Down through the years, I realized that prayer really works. Those who don't believe me should try it and find out for themselves.

As I headed north to once again be with my family, I looked forward to seeing them, but I had an empty feeling about leaving the friends I had made the last three years.

CHAPTER ELEVEN
THE LAST STEPS

I left the service, took a short trip to Milwaukee to visit with the Knott family, then continued on to Foster City. It was nice to be home again, but I knew I wouldn't stay long. I wasn't sure what I wanted to do, and I had no real training. I hadn't taken advantage of the various schools offered to me in the air force.

Before deciding what to do concerning my future, I agreed to take a trip out West with my sisters, Ann and Ruth, and Ann's daughter, Roxanne. When I returned from the service, I had thought I might like to live in San Francisco. It sounded good, and since I had never been there, I had no idea what it would be like. Sometimes, when a person is uncertain, it is like grabbing at straws.

In early September, we started our vacation along the northern route. Our first stop was the Badlands, then we visited Mount Rushmore. Until a person stands at the foot of that mountain, it's impossible to visualize how big the presidents' heads really are and the work that must have gone into carving them for generations to enjoy another part of American history. Next, we traveled to Custer's Last Stand.

As I stood there looking down at the battlefield, I wondered how it must have been for him and his men as they faced certain death. I guess people will never know what went through his mind the last few hours of his life and the lives of the men who so courageously followed him. I wondered how I would face death when my turn came. Would I look it in the eye, or would I try to run?

Of course, we couldn't miss Yellowstone National Park, which is another great wonder of the world. Old Faithful was breathtaking, as were the other beautiful sites in the park. The wildlife roamed, living as they wanted. God had truly blessed our country with all that beauty. We were stopped by a few bears, who had decided to check out our car by climbing over it. We were smart enough to stay in the car with the windows rolled up. It was fun watching them so closely. They were always looking for something to eat and people actually got out of their cars to try to be friendly with them. Of course, bears are wild animals, and people shouldn't do that. That's why there are accidents, and the bears are punished rather than the people who invade their territory. The bears have to be removed from their territory or put to death through no fault of their own. We drove on to Salt Lake City to see the Great Salt Lake and Salt Flats. We could see the salt for miles. (Nothing like being the salt of the earth!) The Salt Flats is where a lot of speed testing is performed, and the flats shift daily. Speed testing was occurring when we stopped by, so we were unable to get near the test site.

Of course, a tourist cannot leave Salt Lake City without visiting the beautiful Mormon Temple. The auditorium is hard to describe. Its acoustics are the best in the world. When a pin was dropped on the stage, we could hear it in the back of the auditorium.

We tried our hand at gambling when we stopped in Reno for an evening. It was the first time any of us had been to Nevada. I enjoyed it. It was different from anything we had done so far on our trip.

Reno is in a category all its own. It is called the city that never sleeps, and I believe it. When the nightlife ends, the day workers get everything ready for another night on The Strip. One thing I noticed was all the wedding chapels on The Strip for quick marriages. Everywhere we stopped was different. All the gambling halls had their own attractions to attract potential customers.

We went to the San Francisco area to visit Dad's brother and his family. They took us around San Francisco, Oakland and vicinity, and then to Fisherman's Wharf. They showed us points of interest such as the zoo to Alcatraz and everything between. There was so much to see, we could not see it all in a few days. In later years, I moved to that area with my husband, but when I was young, I did not want to stay. It was a scary place for me at that point in my life, even if I did have an uncle and sunt living there.

We quickly decided to complete the trip. We said our good-byes, thanked them for a wonderful time, and headed south.

We arrived in Southern California, and our first stop was Knott's Berry Farm. All the places were interesting in their own way. We are at some of the best eating places in the area and took a few rides, but not like those at Disneyland, which was our next stop, then Marine World.

The four of us enjoyed the same activities, which made it nice. The only difference we had was getting up in the morning. Ruthie was always the early bird, while Anna and I liked to sleep. So, Ruthie was always getting us up; otherwise, things were great.

We spent an afternoon and evening at Disneyland. We had fun on the rides, even if we did have to stand in line. We saw shows and exhibits. The evening was beautiful; the park was all lit up. I enjoyed the president's exhibit the most. It was so lifelike. It was as if we were actually in the early part of history. Disneyland closed, and we, too, were ready for a good night's sleep. We walked toward our car to head back to the hotel, but, lo and behold,

we couldn't find the vehicle! We hadn't realized there were so many parking lots, and we didn't remember in which lot we had left it! So, after the park closed and most of the cars were gone, the caretakers were kind enough to drive us around the lots in their Jeep to help us find the car. After a few rounds, there it was, right where we had left it! It was not two in the morning. The incident was funny later, but at the time we were riding around looking for the car it wasn't so funny. At least we didn't think so.

We visited Marine World the next day. The shows were breathtaking. It was amazing to see what the whales, sharks, and porpoises could do. After each act, they received treats as rewards for jobs well done. The seals had personalities all their own. By the time we had watched a few shows and seen the exhibits, it was late, so we decided to top off the evening by going out to eat.

We decided to eat at a fancy restaurant, so we returned to the hotel to dress in our finest, new purses and all. We each had only one set of dress clothes, but that was plenty. Each time we dressed up, we were in a different town.

We had a few drinks and one of the most enjoyable meals of the trip. We ended the lovely evening, and when it came time to pay, we opened our purses and didn't have fifty cents between us. If ever people were embarrassed, we were. We had brought our new purses and hadn't bothered to transfer our things from the old to the new. There we were with our new purses and nothing in them! We didn't even have our drivers' licenses.

Anna was willing to leave her watch while we returned to the hotel to get the money. She was the only one with a watch of any value. The manager was very understanding, and he told us to pay the bill in the morning on our way out of town. The next morning, we returned to pay the bill, and he was very surprised. He had thought he would never see us again since some people do that sort of thing intentionally. It made us feel good inside that we went back and paid the bill instead of leaving town without paying. It gives us a good feeling to pay our bills in life and not let them fall by the wayside. Somebody else has to pay if we don't.

We headed home on Highway 66, which is no longer Highway 66. Now it's an interstate highway from California to Michigan with four different numbers. Our route took us through the desert. It, too, had its beauty and was different than anything we had seen. When the sunset, it was breathtaking. Amidst all the beauty stood the California missions. Many were as busy as ever; others were rundown and not in use anymore. They had fallen victim to many passersby through the early years and were a refuge for others.

The desert was pretty, but it bloomed mostly in the spring. At that time, it is the most beautiful even in September, however, the desert was lovely.

We left California and traveled through Arizona, then New Mexico. We visited the most beautiful caverns in the world at Carlsbad. The colors were unbelievable, and at the end of the tour, the walls of the caverns lit up with the American flag. Each place we visited had a beauty of its own.

We stopped at the Alamo, deep in the heart of Texas. The Alamo gave us another example of bravery. The men who fought there had not been able to walk away, even when it meant certain death to their brave souls. With just a handful of men, they held off Santa Anna's troops for days. It was events like the Alamo that made our country great, so we should continue to stand up for what we believe. Through the years, each generation has risen to the occasion, and that's what makes our country great.

After a month or so on the road, we returned to Milwaukee, which was where I got off. Roxanne, Ann, and Ruth went on to Niagara, then Foster City. In the meantime, I rented a room at the YMCA. I stayed there a few months. Jobs were hard to find, but by that time, I had more confidence, even if I didn't have any special skills. Doing office work and playing sports in the air force didn't exactly prepare me for the future. My first job was working through a temporary employment agency, and I was able to go to many parts of the city. I learned about the various ways offices were run for different companies, but I didn't care about office work. The jobs lasted from one day to weeks, and I did enjoy moving around like that; however, I still had my eye on moving on to something else.

I read a travel magazine that I had checked out of the library. There was still so much to do and see as far as I was concerned, and I wanted it all. I guess I was afraid of getting into a rut and remaining there for twenty years or more. I knew there was nothing wrong with that, if that was what a person wanted, and back in the 1950s and 1960s, that was the thing to do.

I believe if people want to go or do something, they shouldn't let other people change their minds as long as they're not hurting anyone or anything in the process.

I missed the air force because I had been active and had made many good friends, some of whom I still keep in contact with after forty years or more. I didn't want to return to the service, however, because I would be put right back in the office again.

One day, while I was reading the daily paper, and an ad caught my eye. It was about becoming a ticket agent or stewardess. The latter position, of course, was out of the picture because of my size. I applied to the airline school in Minneapolis. I took the test and was accepted. I think most people who took the test were accepted because it wasn't hard.

The training course was only ten weeks long, but I had to go to Minneapolis. I stayed with a very nice lady whose name I got through the school. It turned out that she was a distant relative, which I found out while staying there. She had a big house, and with all her children grown, she was by herself. We were good company for each other. I helped around the house and shoveled snow for her, which was a job in itself. Anyone who has been to Minneapolis in the winter knows what I'm talking about.

There wasn't a lot to the school, but we learned about the different airlines. As it turned out, the school did not have a good track record when it came to helping its students find a job. I got to know many people, however, but none of them became close friends.

I didn't want to remain in Minneapolis. Three months there was enough for me. It was too cold and windy. Minneapolis did have a good bus system, however, and I used it a lot, but once again, I was ready to move on, and that's what I did.

I went to Chicago, which wasn't any better. The weather in Chicago was just as bad, if not worse than in Minneapolis. It seemed as if I got cold in the fall and stayed that way until spring. In the summer it was too hot with its high humidity. The weather in Chicago went from one extreme to another.

I stayed with my aunt, Lillian Carlson. She wasn't really my aunt, but she was like one of the family. I guess everyone has someone who isn't a blood relative but is considered a relative anyway. That's how I felt about Lillian and her husband, Herbert. They had no children, and I stayed with them about nine or ten months. My one and only job in Chicago was not with an airline but with a bank in downtown Chicago. It was a big bank, and I worked the second shift. We posted accounts, etc. I didn't care for the job, but I needed a paycheck, so I stayed six months or so. I knew there were jobs out there just for me and all I had to do was find one. I still wanted to travel and be part of something, so my thoughts went back to the military. Deep inside, I wanted to go back.

By that time, the army was enlisting people and letting them pick their own career field, which seemed to be just what I was seeking. So, once again, I went to the recruiting office to check it out.

How could I pick the career I wanted? That took some thought, since there were so many careers forms which to choose.

I signed up for communications as a Teletype operator, and that's the training I got. The recruiters kept their word. This time, however, I was in the army instead of the air force because the air force would give me only office work since that's what I had done before. The army allowed me to travel more and to go overseas, which was one of my dreams that had come true in later years.

As I close the pages on this part of my life, I sit and think, once again, about the first time I went into the air force and then into the army.

Lillian and Herbert were very nice to me and gave me a going away party. I felt good when I was around them because I wasn't overshadowed by anything or anybody. I remember Herbert liked to argue about religion. He thought it was fun. I never argued about it; however, when Ruthie came to visit, she got into an argument every time. Neither won, but I guess they enjoyed it.

Lillian was sick at that time, so I stayed with her during the day and Herbert stayed with her at night. They never got along well, which, I guess, is why they enjoyed a third person in the house. That way they always had someone with whom to talk. I was always in the middle of things. They also kept everything they bought. I often wondered how they moved everything when they migrated to Florida years later.

I went shopping for Lillian all the time, and she liked to go to two or three places to buy things. After awhile, I got smart and bought everything in one store. I put in the extra money so I wouldn't have to go all over town. I was in Chicago, remember.

When Lillian saw in the paper that a bank or savings company was offering free gifts to people starting a new account, she would draw her money out of one bank and put it in the new one to receive the free gift. She had a lot of ideas about how to get things. If she couldn't use them herself, she gave them as gifts.

Now, as this part of my life comes to a close, I think of my family, of what they have been through and what the future has in store for them. It's better I don't know, or I would worry.

I think I was fortunate to grow up in Foster City, but the most important element in my life was being a part of the Swanson family. We had roots. We knew where we were and where we came from. Many people do not know their own parents, sisters, or brothers until years later.

All my sisters and brothers helped to mold my life, whether they meant to or not. We were a part of each other, and when we traveled through life, we took a little of each other with us.

The Bible says that when you are older, you shall return to the ways of your youth.

We grew up to love and respect each other, and things seemed to go pretty well for all of us as we went our separate ways. Even if we didn't see each other very often, we still kept in touch. I knew they were there if I needed them, and that fact meant a lot to me.

As the years passed, sadness overshadowed the Swanson family again with the sudden death of Marion. She was in her early forties. She left behind a husband, Kenneth, and three teenage children. I really missed her letters, which had been filled with advice and encouragement during the years I was away from home. With changes and the passing of time, things never remain the same. Sometimes I wished I could turn back time to escape times like that, but I knew it couldn't be done that way.

I realize we have to go through the valleys before we enjoy the mountaintops. With God's help we will all make it through the valleys.

Marion was a big part of the community of Foster City. It showed when the townspeople paid their last respect and when Marion was laid to rest. She, too, was ready to meet her Lord. She always told me that we had to be ready when our time came.

Time marched on, and another person dear to us passed away, Arnin's husband, Dr. Mac, as he was called by the people of Niagara, whom he faithfully served for many years. I didn't know him very well because I had already left home and was on my own in Milwaukee when he married Ann, but when I visited them those few times, I enjoyed the visit. He, too, was well respected in the town of Niagara and the outlying communities. He was citizen of the year for the state of Wisconsin a few years before. He was a kind doctor who never said no, the breed of doctor we just don't see today. Whether someone had money or not, he treated them like a person. If a patient couldn't pay a bill in money, he accepted an animal or whatever they wanted to give him in place of cash. If the patient didn't have either, that would be okay, too. Sometimes he would have two or three animals at a time in his front yard.

The shadow appeared again in 1988 when I received a call from Ann to tell me Dad had cancer. In late January, John and Ann gave Dad a surprise eightieth birthday party. His friends and family attended, which made him feel good even if he didn't want to admit it. He knew he had cancer and was not expected to live.

Dad meant so much to all of us. He was always in my prayers, and I am sure we were always in his through the years. I thought he might win that battle, too, as he had won others in the past. I thanked God that Johnny and Anna were by his side when he needed someone the most. In times like that, Johnny and Anna may never have realized how important they really were to him. Wally, Ruthie, and I went to visit him, but it was John and Ann who carried most of the burden. They were with him on a day-to-day basis.

In March, my husband and I made a trip to Niagara to visit Dad. It was the last time we would see him. He was staying with Ann because he was unable to live alone. When I walked into his room, I was never so taken aback. He was so pale and thin. I had remembered him as a healthy person who was able to care for himself, but he wasn't that person anymore. We all know that it's in times like that when we really need someone around.

Dad and I had the nicest visits, just he and I. As I sat by his bed, we talked, and he never once felt sorry for himself. I knew he had something that many will never have, a special peace with God. He didn't have a bank account, his car was old and worn out, but at times like that it didn't matter.

Dad was our strength through our youth. He had never kissed us goodnight, and he had very seldom hugged us, but we knew how he felt about us. He and I would have a good supper together, then he would go to bed. I would sit and read the paper to him or just wait until he went to sleep.

Sometimes we wouldn't exchange more than a word or two for hours, but just our being together meant a lot to me. We talked about the future, what was in store for him, and about how I shouldn't cry when he was gone. It was hard to keep back the tears when I sat with him. Like it was when Mom passed away, his passing took a part of us.

As time goes by, I'm beginning to understand the many things we had talked about, things we had never talked about before. I thanked God for helping us to make that trip, which was the last time I saw him. I wasn't able to return home for the funeral, but I was there in spirit. One of the last things Dad said to me was, "We all have burdens to bear. Don't blame someone else. for your burdens. Take care of yourself."

www.ingramcontent.com/pod-product-compliance
Lightning Source LLC
Chambersburg PA
CBHW031523120626
46545CB00005B/1972